"What if you live where you live not because you got a good deal to purchase or rent but rather because God has intentionally placed you there to seek its common good? *The Hopeful Neighborhood* weaves together engaging stories, biblical insight, historical context, relevant research, and practical steps to help the reader participate in what God seeks to do in their community. Read and put this book into practice, and we will see the kingdom come in our neighborhoods as it is in heaven."

**Dana Allin,** synod executive, ECO: A Covenant Order of Evangelical Presbyterians

"*The Hopeful Neighborhood* is a critical read for anyone desiring to rebuild the social fabric of our communities. Change won't come from institutional leaders but from those on the street willing to do the hard work of listening, honoring our commonalities, and advancing good."

**Gabe Lyons,** president, Q Media, author of *Good Faith* and *unChristian*

"The most accessible and the most promising mission field might be our neighborhood. Yet most Christians do not know their neighbors. Our individualism and consumerism have kept us isolated. In this third book in Everts's trilogy with Lutheran Hour Ministries and Barna Group, we get a very helpful picture of how we might embrace the common good of what is nearest to us. Everts brings us into lively discussion with Scripture and church history to offer a very promising picture of where we might engage in God's call to us."

**Jim Singleton,** Gordon-Conwell Theological Seminary

"Put *The Hopeful Neighborhood* into practice, and you'll discover any grief you feel about the decline of the institutional church will be replaced by lively hope. In today's America, ringing church bells no longer compel most people to come to worship, but worshipers joining others to pursue the common good in their neighborhood creates opportunities to share the hope that is in us. Interestingly, the majority of God's Ten Commandments are about others, about seeking the common good of people. Don Everts invites us to see that old truth anew."

**Dale Meyer,** president of Concordia Seminary

"Once again, Don Everts and the Barna team have partnered to create a book that enlightens and challenges. For a people who have been living 'above place,' *The Hopeful Neighborhood* is both an invitation and a guide to being rooted. It draws on Scripture, the history of the early church, current research, and real-life examples to illumine an alternative way of life for the common good. Your neighbors probably need this book . . . to be read by you!"

**John Ortberg,** pastor and author

# THE Hopeful NEIGHBORHOOD

## WHAT HAPPENS WHEN CHRISTIANS PURSUE THE COMMON GOOD

## DON EVERTS

Foreword by DAVID KINNAMAN

An imprint of InterVarsity Press
Downers Grove, Illinois

*InterVarsity Press*
*P.O. Box 1400, Downers Grove, IL 60515-1426*
*ivpress.com*
*email@ivpress.com*

*InterVarsity Press® is the book-publishing division of InterVarsity Christian Fellowship/USA®, a movement of students and faculty active on campus at hundreds of universities, colleges, and schools of nursing in the United States of America, and a member movement of the International Fellowship of Evangelical Students. For information about local and regional activities, visit intervarsity.org.*

*Scripture quotations, unless otherwise noted, are from The Holy Bible, English Standard Version, copyright © 2001 by Crossway Bibles, a division of Good News Publishers. Used by permission. All rights reserved.*

*All figures, unless otherwise noted, designed by Annette Allen, data visualizations developed by Alyce Youngblood and Traci Hochmuth, Barna Group, copyright Lutheran Hour Ministries.*

*While any stories in this book are true, some names and identifying information may have been changed to protect the privacy of individuals.*

*Cover design and image composite: Cindy Kiple*
*Interior design: Jeanna Wiggins*
*Images: gated community illustration: © Imagezoo / Getty Images*
*compass and map: © nicoolay / E+ / Getty Images*
*compass: © bortonia / DigitalVision Vectors / Getty Images*

*ISBN 978-0-8308-4803-4 (print)*
*ISBN 978-0-8308-4804-1 (digital)*

*Printed in the United States of America ♾*

*InterVarsity Press is committed to ecological stewardship and to the conservation of natural resources in all our operations. This book was printed using sustainably sourced paper.*

**Library of Congress Cataloging-in-Publication Data**
*A catalog record for this book is available from the Library of Congress.*

**P**  *21  20  19  18  17  16  15  14  13  12  11  10  9  8  7  6  5  4  3  2  1*

**Y**  *38  37  36  35  34  33  32  31  30  29  28  27  26  25  24  23  22  21  20*

To

all the neighbors

God has given me—

past, present, and future

# Contents

# Foreword

**DAVID KINNAMAN**
*President, Barna Group*

I know dozens of people in my family and among close friends who will want to read this book—who will be getting this book as a gift from me. (Jeff, for one, you're welcome.) *The Hopeful Neighborhood* grapples—in some of the most clear and accessible writing that I've yet read—with some of the questions and concerns that I've been hearing for years.

Helping Christians to live in natural, normal, and God-honoring ways *in our communities* is a big challenge in the church today. How do we genuinely demonstrate our faith in Jesus in the places where we live and to the people who live near us? After years of research at Barna Group, I am convinced that getting Christians to have a framework for living their faith locally—for being contributors to a hopeful neighborhood—is not only a challenge but a significant opportunity.

We let a lot of things hinder us in this regard. I believe we are burdened sometimes by the weight of the negative perceptions of Christians. We often live into the stereotypes that sadly we've helped to create: hypocritical, judgmental, more concerned about policies than people, sheltered. I've written a lot about these kinds of barriers with my friend Gabe Lyons (in books called *unChristian* and *Good Faith*). Christians are perceived to be irrelevant (we are unseen and unimportant) or worse, extreme (we are perceived to prioritize the wrong things that bring harm and hate to our communities).

But there is a way to shift those perceptions in a biblical, Christ-honoring way—by being part of a hopeful neighborhood.

Another barrier, which I see in the data all the time, is that churches and pastors are often complicit in keeping Christians *church*bound. What I mean is that, for good motives and good reasons, a type of bargain is offered to keep Christians volunteering, serving, and giving in and through the local church. This isn't all bad; the most resilient kinds of disciples are active and involved in and through their local churches.

Yet the most resilient of Christians are, in addition to their church engagement, also active in the world where God has placed them; they deeply concern themselves with poverty; they work to reverse injustices; they bring their soul with them to their workplaces; they contribute to hopeful neighborhoods.

Finally, the most concerning barrier to loving and serving in the places where we live is fear. We don't want to say the wrong thing. We don't want to be known for our frailties and faults. We are afraid of putting something at risk in our own lives—our time, our reputations, our hearts, our priorities. We are not so sure we want to follow a Jesus who asks us to wash others' feet and get our hands dirty.

Still, the most hopeful neighborhoods are filled with people who believe that perfect love casts out fear. We can be those kinds of Christians, trusting in a God who says he does not traffic in fear but in love, power, and sound minds.

This book does such a beautiful job of preparing us for life on mission with Jesus in the place where we live and with the people who live near us, in our neighborhoods. And my friend Don shares so much of his own journey—he's lived in thirty neighborhoods! He lovingly, carefully, persuasively guides us through the barriers to engaging and loving our neighbors as Christ calls. I hope you gain as much from the journey as I have.

# Introduction

## LIVING ABOVE PLACE

My family and I live in the Pierremont neighborhood found in the subtle hills west of St. Louis.

When we moved into Pierremont twelve years ago, my wife Wendy and I did what came naturally to us as hospitable former missionary types—we went around to meet our new neighbors. This was mostly a pleasant and casual process until I met my next-door neighbor Michael for the first time.

I saw Michael working on his immaculate yard as I pulled into my driveway a week or so after we moved in. I waved and walked over to introduce myself. We shook hands and exchanged names and pleasantries—but as we did so, Michael got a sort of puzzled expression on his face. I found out why when he looked in my eyes and said, "You know, Don, you're the first person on this block to ever shake my hand."

"What?" I replied, "How long have you lived here?"

"Over twenty years," Michael responded, nodding his head and looking thoughtful.

And thus began a pretty deep forty-five-minute conversation about Michael's story in particular and about neighbors in general. I began to look at my new neighborhood, Pierremont, differently after that conversation.

Wendy and I continued to do our hospitality thing with vigor: we had neighbor families over for dinner (including Michael and his family), and our driveway and double garage became a knockabout area for our own kids and all the neighborhood kids as well. In the midst of all the good of Pierremont (Halloween is like one big block party) and all the bad of Pierremont (smoldering feuds between neighbors are not pretty), I remained saddened that someone could go decades in this neighborhood with no neighbor coming over to shake their hand. And I remained convicted that as for me and my family, we were going to be a blessing in our neighborhood.

Then something unexpected happened.

We began to disengage from our neighborhood. This wasn't a purposeful or quick thing. It's just that slowly, over time, we became more absorbed in our church and our jobs and our kids' activities, which increasingly had little or nothing to do with Pierremont. I didn't know it at the time or even have the language to describe it, but Wendy, our kids, and I were increasingly "living above place"—living our lives relatively detached from the place and people right around our home.

It turns out this is an increasingly common experience.[1] But it took a cross-country trip and a great novel to help me realize it was happening with us, and to begin to wonder whether I was okay with that.

## SWARMED IN A HAY MAZE

The trip was to Franklin, Tennessee. I went there to attend a funky little Christian conference called Hutchmoot. The novel was *Jayber Crow*, a rural tale written by Christian farmer and essayist Wendell Berry. I bought the novel at the conference bookstore and snuck away to a nearby hay maze during a break to get a little reading time and some needed solitude.

I was sitting on a dilapidated lawn chair in the exact center of the hay maze when I began reading this story of town barber Jayber Crow and his relationship to the place and people around him—the fictional river town of Port William, Kentucky. Berry's novel is a vehicle for him to express his deep, human, Christian convictions about the importance of our relationship to the place and people around us.

Sitting in the middle of that hay maze I realized how hungry I was for just that. Berry's rich description of Jayber's steady connection to the place and people around him (Berry calls this web of interconnectedness "the membership") made me realize how disconnected I had become from the place and people around me—my Pierremont neighborhood.

> The membership: all the interconnected and interdependent parts of a place, including the people, the land, and all the creatures.

Sitting in that hay maze I began to realize how Wendy, the kids, and I had begun "living above place," and I wasn't sure how I felt about that. What Berry was describing in the novel felt so right to me, both as a human and as a Christian. And how I was living felt a bit wrong. As I sat in that fraying lawn chair, questions began to invade the hay maze like a swarm of locusts:

- Was Berry being overly idealistic?
- Is it even possible to experience "the membership" in a subdivision?
- When Jesus said "love your neighbor," did that include our literal neighbors?
- Did God create humans to be in relationship with the place and people around them?
- Did God call his people to relate to the place and people around them *in a certain way*?
- Should Wendy and the kids and I move to a small river town in Kentucky?
- Did this neighborly instinct get stunted in me because I moved so much when I was growing up?
- Is commuting evil?
- What does Jesus think about me and my neighborhood?
- Can you reengage with neighbors after mostly ignoring them for years?

■ Is there anyone else in Pierremont who hasn't had their hand shaken?

These swarming questions were wonderful and heady and pesky and annoying all at the same time. I swatted them away like I would any buzzing summer insect. But here's the thing: when I walked out of the hay maze, those questions followed me. They kept buzzing around my head, pesky and fascinating and persistent. They followed me on that long drive home back to my house in the slightly hilly subdivision west of St. Louis called Pierremont.

## LOOKING FOR ANSWERS

And thus began a journey for me. This journey was fueled by a profound curiosity: As Christians how should we interact with the place and people around us? What kind of relationship should we have with our neighborhoods?

This journey involved a fair amount of study. I dove into all parts of the Scriptures, into the pages of church history, into the writings of thoughtful Christians in topics like community development and urbanism and sociology and theology and mission and evangelism and farming and ecology. These various areas of study got me into all sorts of helpful conversations with experts and friends, family members and colleagues.

This journey also involved brand new research. I've had the privilege of working with sharp, thoughtful Christians at

Lutheran Hour Ministries and the Barna Group in doing new research on a different important topic each year for the last few years. First, we researched the important topic of spiritual conversations, exploring how to winsomely and fruitfully share the good news of Jesus in conversation with others. (To find out what we learned, see my book *The Reluctant Witness.*[2]) In year two we pulled out from individuals to study whole households of faith, exploring how the Christian faith is nurtured and passed on within our homes. (Check out *The Spiritually Vibrant Home* to explore what we learned.[3])

Over this last year we pulled out from households to research the relationship between Christians and their neighborhoods. In this third study we asked, How do Christians relate to the place and people around them, and How are Christians perceived by their neighbors? (The major statistical findings of this research can be found in our monograph for leaders, *Better Together: How Christians Can Be a Welcome Influence in Their Neighborhoods.*[4]) This third year of research rests on and presumes the findings from the first two years of research where we explored the importance of spiritual conversations and our households. In the same way, my own neighborhood journey may have been sparked at that hay maze, but it has been informed and shaped, in important ways, by what these first two research studies taught me about sharing my faith in conversation and nurturing the faith in my household.

## NOMADS AND NEIGHBORHOODS

But my own journey didn't end with study and research alone, it has also involved a deep season of introspection. The question sounds simple enough: How should Christians relate to the place and people around them? But this isn't a theoretical question, it cuts to the heart of the story of my own life.

As I reflect on my own life story I feel simultaneously that I am the last person who should be bringing these research findings to light and that maybe my own story qualifies me in unique ways to do just that.

On the one hand, I don't have deep roots in any neighborhood. I've lived a relatively nomadic life: living in eleven different neighborhoods while growing up and another twelve as an adult. The longest I've spent in any one neighborhood is the twelve years I've lived in Pierremont. I just haven't experienced the long haul in any one neighborhood like Jayber Crow experienced in Port William. In other words, I'm no neighborhood expert.

Neighborhood: "the place where you live and sleep—it could be your block or the square mile where you live. It may or may not have a name."[5]

On the other hand, I have experienced many different neighborhoods. I've lived in ten houses, six apartment complexes, three duplexes, two dorm rooms, one condo, and a trailer. I did the math and discovered I've lived in twenty-three different neighborhoods. Throw in seven other neighborhoods where I spent entire summers and I've gotten to live in *thirty distinct neighborhoods* during my life: some rural, some urban, some suburban. So perhaps I do have a type of neighborhood expertise.

At the very least, I can honestly say I have been personally wrestling with the very topic I and my partners have been studying and researching. Along the way I've been surprised by what I have read in the Bible (a book I like to think I'm fairly well acquainted with) and encouraged by the research (it turns out people want to make a difference in their neighborhoods and are looking for help in figuring out how to do that).

I've become increasingly convinced that significant hope is on the horizon for Christians and their neighborhoods throughout our country. It seems to me that in a day of isolation and loneliness, a simple path to relationship lies right in front of us. In a day of division, a path to unity lies right in front of us. And in a day when Christians and the church are being dismissed as irrelevant, a path to relevance lies right in front of us.

There is nothing new about this path, of course. Based on what is revealed in God's Word and shown throughout church history I believe it is an ancient path that God is calling us to take: to pursue the common good of the place and people around us. And that's exactly what this book is about.

## THE HOPEFUL NEIGHBORHOOD

In chapter one, "Pursue the Common Good," we will explore what is so exciting (and important) about Christians pursuing this thing called "the common good" of their neighborhood. What does the Bible have to say about the common good, and what has that meant for God's people throughout history?

In chapter two, "Use Every Gift," we will explore a simple but revolutionary process for pursuing the common good that has always been right there in God's Word, even though we often default to a quite different (fairly unhealthy) process.

When God's people are living through difficult times they are most tempted to isolate themselves from their neighbors, but their pursuit of the common good can be the most revolutionary and powerful. In chapter three, "Love Everyone Always," we will look at this historical trend and practical implications for our current season.

Inevitably, any exploration of Christians' pursuit of the common good must come around to spiritual matters. It's one thing to love a neighbor with art or a conversation or a meal, but what about their spiritual needs? In this matter the Bible and history are unambiguous: Christians' good works in their neighborhoods bring glory to God. We explore these joyful dynamics in chapter four, "Give God Glory."

Finally, in chapter five, "Join the Revolution," we'll take a careful look at how important networks are in our pursuit of the common good. It turns out God has called us to such a grand mission that there's no option but to partner with others in accomplishing it.

## A PATH TO HOPE

This is the path that *The Hopeful Neighborhood* will take you on. Along the way you will encounter lots of Scripture, stories of everyday Christians from hundreds of years ago and today, and brand new research from the Barna Group. You'll also find some fiction, reflection and discussion questions, stories from my own life, and immediate practical steps—creative elements to help us not just learn something new but *contemplate* (and maybe even act on) what we are learning.

And so if you are tired of "living above place" and find yourself hungry for a more grounded and integrated life, keep reading. You may find that there is a way to bring the disparate pieces of your life together, no matter how long you've lived in your neighborhood.

If you are tired of the culture wars and find yourself hungry for a more kind and respectful way of influencing the world around you, keep reading. You may find that there is a more loving and effective way to change culture.

If you are tired of the church being dismissed as irrelevant and find yourself hungry for a compelling, attractive Christian presence in our country, keep reading. You may find that this ancient path can take the church back to the center of your community.

If you are tired of a consumer-oriented faith and find yourself hungry to create and bless and use the gifts God has given you to help others, keep reading. You may find that God has equipped every one of us with powerful gifts that are key to our neighborhoods.

If you are tired of being isolated in a Christian holy huddle and find yourself hungry for more real relationships with non-Christians, keep reading. You may find that you and your non-Christian neighbors have more in common than you think.

And if you are tired of despair, if you are tired of gloomy culture watchers who lament how the cause of Christianity is on an unrelenting downward spiral and find yourself hungry for some good news, keep reading. You may encounter what I have encountered during this journey: hope.

Hope is, after all, our birthright as followers of Jesus—no matter what neighborhood we live in.

# Pursue the Common Good

## THE SHARED WORK OF ALL HUMANS

*The LORD God took the man and put him in the garden of Eden to work it and keep it.*

**GENESIS 2:15**

I was living in an apartment complex on the outskirts of Knoxville, Tennessee, when I first felt the weight of our common humanity. I was in first grade and the events of a single month in our apartment complex confronted my young heart with both the joys and horrors of our shared humanity.

First grade was a time of important firsts for me: I was introduced to Fruit Stripe gum and Star Wars action figures and the ins and outs of papier-mâché. But the whole common humanity realization (at least the joyful part) was triggered by an invitation from my teacher, Mrs. Love. She knew that one of the girls in my class lived in the same apartment complex that I did. She also knew (I realize in retrospect) that I was struggling to make friends in class and that my classmate was struggling with her reading. And so, the invitation: Would we spend an hour reading together when we got home from school each day?

And that's exactly what we did. It felt as right as rain to sit together after school and take turns reading out loud from the same book. My older brother and sister sometimes lingered in the living room to hear the stories too. And not only did I enjoy reading and making a friend, but after a few weeks of this we got an unforgettable reminder of how important this kind of partnership was.

I remember Mrs. Love got everyone's attention in class for "an important lesson," having us all sit crisscross applesauce on the large classroom rug. The gist of her lesson: *we are all in this together*. Mrs. Love told us that we first graders were here to have fun and learn *as a class*. We were like a team. We were partners. And then she told everyone about my new friend's and my afterschool reading partnership, and then (I could hardly believe what was happening) she invited my neighbor and me to visit the Treasure Box!

Mrs. Love kept a Treasure Box behind her desk, which was filled with all manner of toys and treats and delights. That Treasure Box occupied a special place in our first-grade minds. And that morning Mrs. Love underscored the joy of partnering together by inviting my new friend and me to each choose one item from the famed Treasure Box. This was my first visit to the

Treasure Box, and the lesson was indelibly marked on my young heart: *we're all in this together*. And that is something worth celebrating.

But then the horror part came. A couple of weeks later the news flew through the apartment complex: a young girl's body had been found in one of the dumpsters in the parking lot. It was *not* my reading buddy. But it was unmistakably *one of us*—another student, surely someone's classmate and partner.

I was so confused. I thought we were all in this together? Why would someone put *one of us* in the dumpster? I'm not sure I completely understood the death part of the situation (let alone the implications about murder) because I remember empathizing with the young girl, wondering what it must have felt like to be thrown away. How uncomfortable it must have been to lie with all the garbage in one of those stinky dumpsters in the parking lot. I was devastated.

This lesson, too, was indelibly marked on my young heart: *we're all in this together*. And sometimes that is a weighty thing. Both the joy and the horror taught me, even in first grade, that I was a part of the human classroom, the partnership of humanity. I learned we were all in this together, and in both joyful and horrible ways that just felt right.

Of course, as I grew older I would feel the temptation to treat people like *others* and feel the small rush and petty elevation that came from treating other people like trash. But when I eventually got around to studying what the Bible has to say

about the making of the human classroom, I discovered that
Mrs. Love had been right back in first grade. We humans are all
in this together, created as partners in a shared work.

## BEAUTIFULLY CREATED TO
## PURSUE THE COMMON GOOD

The opening chapters of the Bible, which are all about the creation of earth and humanity and all that is, are unambiguous:
all humans are created by God. God is the source of all life on
earth, including all humans. There is only one Creator, and
therefore all humans are fellow creations.

This much is commonly known. But when you spend unhurried time hanging out in the first pages of the Bible, you are
likely to stumble upon a surprising fact of life in the Garden of
Eden that has always been staring us in the face: humans were
given work to do. As we read in Genesis: "The LORD God took
the man and put him in the garden of Eden to work it and keep
it" (Genesis 2:15).

The wording here implies that the land needed someone to
cultivate it for it to be useful and habitable.[1] "Gardens cannot
look after themselves; they are not self-perpetuating."[2] Rather,
they need someone to *work* them and *keep* them. These are
interesting words used to characterize our shared human work.

First, God placed humans here on earth to work the land
where we are standing. The Hebrew here literally means to
"serve" the land, implying that we humans are designed to serve

the place where we live, not be served by it.[3] Second, humans are created to "keep" the place around us. This Hebrew word is rich in meaning, signifying "to take care of something" or even "to exercise great care" over something.[4]

Humans, the Bible tells us, are placed here on earth to serve and care for the place around us. This is humanity's creation mandate.[5] This mandate included caring for the land itself but also all the creatures residing within that land. Not to mention the other people around us! In other words, we humans were designed to stand shoulder to shoulder and put our hands to the same shared work: pursuing the common good.

> Common good = "the flourishing or well-being of the sum total of communal life in a given place."[6]

The *common good* of a place is similar to Wendell Berry's concept of "the membership"—it includes everything about the place and people around you. Pursuing the collective good of the land and animals and structures and people and relationships around us affirms "the sense of community solidarity that binds all in a common destiny" and seems to be the task for which humans were placed on earth.[7] God placed humanity on earth for this shared work: "managing all of its creatures and resources for *good* purposes: to allow their beauty to flourish, to use them wisely and kindly, and to promote well-being for all."[8]

This creation mandate shows us the great dignity and value imbued in humans: we aren't mere creatures. We are entrusted with an important, beautiful calling: to create and shape "an environment where creatures can flourish."[9] This shared human pursuit isn't limited to the making of good names and good crops and good people (as we see explicitly in the Genesis text) but would also include the making of *any good, true, and beautiful thing* that promotes the common good, including, eventually, a good meal, a good house, a good conversation, a good song, a good analysis, even a good organization or department or meeting.

It bears noting that this isn't just work for Christians, of course. Every human being is dignified and empowered with this creation mandate to work and keep the place around them, to pursue the common good. This creation mandate to pursue the common good is universal and is the most distinctive thing we humans do.[10] As I learned in first grade, we humans are all in this together.

## Paradigm Shift
### FROM NEIGHBORS TO CONSUMERS

There has been a paradigm shift going on in neighborhoods in the United States since the end of WWII. For decades before the 1940s, neighborhoods were places where people were known and were active. Whether a rural community, a suburban street, an urban block, or an apartment complex, neighbors commonly saw themselves as having a shared life in their neighborhood that naturally involved celebrating together, helping each other, and looking after the neighborhood.

But that's been changing. The evidence suggests that "America's dramatic economic growth during the post-WWII era has been accompanied by substantial increases in individualism and materialism."[a] We may be experiencing unprecedented levels of prosperity, but our social fabric is falling apart.[b] While our GNP (Gross National Product) has been doing quite well, our GNH (Gross National Happiness) has not. The GNH is an index of seventy-two indicators that seek to measure well-being and flourishing, and our country's GNH has been dropping steadily.[c] Research shows we have lower self-reported happiness, poorer interpersonal relationships, higher levels of anxiety and depression, and greater antisocial behavior.[d] As we focus more on material things and less on relationship,[e] chronic loneliness has become more common in our neighborhoods.[f] And because we are more isolated from our neighbors, we have turned to purchasing the care we once received from neighbors.[g] The net result: neighborhoods are no longer places where we are known and active.

Given what we read in Genesis 1 about our shared work of pursuing the common good, it would seem obvious that this is a paradigm shift that we Christians should evaluate and even actively resist. Regardless of the flow of culture around us, we know that we and all our neighbors were not placed on earth to be isolated consumers but rather to put our hands, with dignity and purpose, to the shared work of pursuing the common good of the place and people around us.

What if we resisted this trend going on around us? What if we started to get to know our neighborhoods (and neighbors) again so that we could be about our shared human task of working and keeping the place right around us?

1. Research indicates that our country is doing better financially but worse socially. What evidence have you seen in your own life or neighborhood that confirms or contradicts these findings?

2. On a scale of 1 to 10, how lonely would you say you are? How lonely would you say your nearest neighbors are?

3. In what ways have you and your neighbors celebrated together, helped each other, or looked after your neighbor together during the last year?

[a]Brian Fikkert and Kelly M. Kapic, *Becoming Whole: Why the Opposite of Poverty Isn't the American Dream* (Chicago: Moody, 2019), 85.

[b]Fikkert and Kapic, *Becoming Whole*, 71.

[c]Fikkert and Kapic, *Becoming Whole*, 83-84.

[d]Fikkert and Kapic, *Becoming Whole*, 85.

[e]Fikkert and Kapic, *Becoming Whole*, 85

[f]Ben Sasse, *Them: Why We Hate Each Other—and How to Heal* (New York: St. Martin's Press: 2018), 24.

[g]Consider that between 1940 and 2010 the US population grew by 134 percent, but the "number of service and therapeutic professionals fulfilling basic life needs rose by 3,206 percent" (Jake Meador, *In Search of the Common Good* [Downers Grove, IL: InterVarsity, 2019], 43).

## EXPLICITLY CALLED TO PURSUE
## THE COMMON GOOD

After humanity's fall into sin, humans lost sight of the shared work God had entrusted to them and their fellow humans. And so, after the fall, God had to explicitly call people to this shared work. The Bible tells us that although Adam was kicked out of the Garden, his mandate to work and keep the land was sent with him: "Therefore the Lord God sent him out from the garden of Eden to work the ground from which he was taken" (Gen 3:23).

Working and keeping the land may have been made more difficult by the curse, but "there is no indication that human dominion over the creation has been rescinded" outside the Garden.[11] Instead, God had to get more explicit in calling humans to this shared task of pursuing the common good. Consider the law God gave his people. In the law there are specific instructions to exercise great care over "the membership" of a place—the land, the people, and all that was in the land.

God's law is explicit about caring for *the land*: for example, there are specifics about maintaining fruit trees (Leviticus 19:23-25), letting the land and fields "rest and lie fallow" every seven years to help the land flourish (Exodus 23:11), and the disposal of human waste (Deuteronomy 23:13-15). God's law was also explicit about caring for *the people* in the land. For example, there are many specifics about not hurting each other but also details about watching out for widows and travelers and orphans in generous ways. God's law also got specific about caring for the *creatures* within the land: addressing resting animals (Deuteronomy 5:14), yoking animals appropriately (Deuteronomy 22:10), avoiding cruelty to animals (Deuteronomy 25:4), and even taking care of your enemy's animals if you see them in need (Exodus 23:4-5).

While we tend to pay more attention (perhaps rightly) to the redemptive elements of the law that deal with humanity's sin and need of reconciliation with God, it is noteworthy that God is still explicit that people are to stand shoulder to shoulder in their original shared work of pursuing the well-being of the place and people around them.

We see this echoed in Jesus' teachings as well. Jesus, who died as an atoning sacrifice for humanity's sins, who made reconciliation with God possible by grace through faith, taught his followers how to then live their everyday lives rooted in this grace they had received. And in his teachings, not only did Jesus call his followers to love their neighbors (Matthew 22:39) and serve the people around them (Matthew 23:11), he also celebrated grace-filled lives that were spent pursuing the common good. As we read in his seminal teaching in the Sermon on the Mount: "Blessed are the peacemakers, for they will be called children of God" (Matthew 5:9 NIV).

Reading an English translation of this blessing may give the impression that Jesus is simply celebrating the practice of nonviolence or the habit of helping others get along and reconcile.

While those activities are included here, this call itself is at once wider and deeper and older than that. You see, it's an interesting word that we read in Jesus' great Sermon on the Mount: *peacemakers*. It's a compound word made up of a word for peace (*eirēnē*) and a word for making (*poieō*).

First, *peace*. The word *peace* means something quite specific—and exciting—coming from the mouth of Jesus. *Eirēnē* is the Greek translation of the Hebrew word *shalom*. Jesus would have understood *shalom* as all Israelites did: as a comprehensive, joyful state of well-being. Shalom is not just the absence of violence (as our English word *peace* tends to connote) but is the presence of all that people need for well-being: safety and security, love and relationships, good work and housing, physical and spiritual health—all of it. God created the world like a fabric of interdependent, knitted, webbed relationships, and this is what the Bible calls shalom.[12] That's the kind of peace Jesus is talking about.

Next, *making*. This word for making is a term that Jesus, as a carpenter, would have been very familiar with. The original word is *poieō*, and it meant to create, make, fashion, or construct. And so this compound word, *peacemakers*, is a description of those people who are engaged with their original shared human task: crafting human flourishing.

What does Jesus have to say about people who do this? They are *blessed* and will be easily recognized as children of God. Jesus is calling his followers to be peacemakers, a call that taps into our ancient, original, shared human work.[13] The latest research conducted by the Barna Group and Lutheran Hour Ministries hints at this *blessedness* that Jesus spoke of.

Researchers isolated a group of people they called "participants"—practicing Christians who had voluntarily gathered

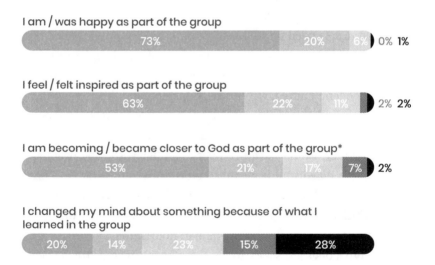

## Personal Outcomes in Successful Groups
*Base: practicing Christian community participants*

● COMPLETELY TRUE  ● MOSTLY TRUE  ● SOMEWHAT TRUE
● A LITTLE TRUE  ● NOT TRUE AT ALL

**I am / was happy as part of the group**
73% | 20% | 6% | 0% | 1%

**I feel / felt inspired as part of the group**
63% | 22% | 11% | 2% | 2%

**I am becoming / became closer to God as part of the group***
53% | 21% | 17% | 7% | 2%

**I changed my mind about something because of what I learned in the group**
20% | 14% | 23% | 15% | 28%

*n*=205 U.S. practicing Christian adults who were part of a group, July 25–August 15, 2019. When answering this question, participants were asked to think about the most successful group they'd been a part of. *For this response, the scale was: strongly agree, somewhat agree, neither agree nor disagree, somewhat disagree, strongly disagree.*

**FIGURE 1.1**

with a group of others to make a difference in the world around them, specifically seeking to make a local impact in the area where they live.[14] These participants were asked to reflect on the various outcomes of any of those groups they considered to be successful.

As you can see in figure 1.1, most of these participants experienced happiness and inspiration and became closer to God because of their involvement in pursuing the common good

## Overlapping Outcomes

**I am happy, and also...**

| | |
|---|---|
| 74% | I made new friends |
| 82% | I feel inspired |
| 71% | We trust one another |
| 70% | We help each other become better |
| 61% | I have become closer to God |

**I have become closer to God, and also...**

| | |
|---|---|
| 84% | I feel happy |
| 81% | I made new friends |
| 83% | I feel inspired |
| 76% | We trust one another |
| 83% | We help each other become better |

FIGURE 1.2

with others. In fact, researchers noted these positive gains "tend to hang together," one benefit begetting others.[15]

For example, "people who say their involvement in a successful group added to their personal happiness are more likely than the average to report every other good outcome."[16] The same synergy of blessings shows up for those who report feeling closer to God, as you can see in figure 1.2. Those who are pursuing the common good really are blessed.

> **1.** When have you felt happier, more inspired, or closer to God after spending time and energy trying to serve someone else?
>
> **2.** What might account for the way one blessing tends to lead to others?
>
> **3.** What are the different costs that can be associated with pursuing the common good of others? How do the potential costs and potential blessings compare?

The earliest Christian leaders repeated Jesus' call to be crafters of peace. For example, Paul issued a call to "pursue what makes for peace" (Romans 14:19) and the author of Hebrews encouraged Christians to "strive for peace" (Hebrews 12:14). James celebrated this same shalom-crafting posture when he wrote that "a harvest of righteousness is sown in peace by those who make peace" (James 3:18).

As it turns out, this is exactly what the first generations of Christians did.

## Pursuing the Common Good Throughout History

Pursuing the common good has been a strong marker of the Christian church from the very beginning.

The early church had many habits that they became known for, of course—including meeting frequently, eating together, and memorizing texts. But they also became known for their relentless pursuit of the common good of their local communities: visiting the poor, the sick, and the imprisoned; receiving and feeding travelers; generously contributing to common funds that went toward caring for the poor, replenishing stocks of food and clothing, and feeding needy people.[a] Christians in the early church busied themselves pursuing the common good of their communities.

Throughout the centuries the church kept talking about this core calling. In The Epistle of Barnabas, an early Christian writing from the end of the first century, we read these words: "Do not live entirely isolated, having retreated into yourselves, as if you were already [fully] justified, but gather instead to seek together the common good."[b]

John Chrysostom, the famed preacher in Constantinople, preached about the common good in the early 400s:

"This is the rule of the most perfect Christianity, its most exact definition, its highest point, namely, the seeking of the common good . . . for nothing can so make a person an imitator of Christ as caring for his neighbors."[c]

From Augustine to Aquinas, from Catholics to Protestants, Christians across the ages and denominations have repeated this call to pursue the common good. As a result, Christians throughout the centuries have stood shoulder to shoulder with the rest of humanity, leaving an enduring positive mark on their world.[d] Any objective historian investigating the effects of Christians throughout history will be overwhelmed with this enduring legacy of shared work throughout society: in the arts, literacy, education, human rights, health care, literature, science, justice, rule of law, and more.[e]

1. Which of the habits of the early church are you most familiar with? Which habits do today's Christians usually focus on?

2. What specific examples of Christians' "enduring legacy" can you think of?

3. How often do you hear Christians today talking about this historically significant Christian habit of "pursuing the common good"?

---

[a]Alan Kreider, *The Patient Ferment of the Early Church: The Improbable Rise of Christianity in the Roman* Empire (Grand Rapids: Baker, 2016), 122-23.

[b]Epistle of Barnabas 4.10, as cited in Michael Lamb and Brian A. Williams, eds., *Everyday Ethics: Moral Theology and the Practices of Ordinary Life* (Washington, DC: Georgetown University Press, 2019), 145.

[c] John Chrysostom quoted in Jim Wallis, *The (Un)Common Good: How the Gospel Brings Hope to a World Divided* (Grand Rapids: Brazos, 2013), 3.

[d] James Davison Hunter, *To Change the World: The Irony, Tragedy, and Possibility of Christianity in the Late Modern World* (New York: Oxford University Press, 2010), 4.

[e] Jonathan Hill, *What Has Christianity Ever Done for Us? How It Shaped the Modern World* (Downers Grove, IL: InterVarsity Press, 2005), 6-7.

While it is true that Christians throughout history have pursued the common good, this shared human work has not always remained at the forefront of the Christian experience. For example, the latest research shows us that people today don't associate Christians with the common good. As can be seen in figure 1.3, when researchers asked people who is best suited to solve problems within their communities only 33 percent of practicing Christians put "churches and Christian organizations" as their top answer to this question, while a mere 7 percent of non-Christians did the same. It is noteworthy that non-Christians see the government and community members as more suited to pursue the common good in their community than groups or organizations of Christians.

**1.** How would you rank the six options given if you were asked who is best suited to solve problems in your neighborhood? How do your answers compare with the averages?

**2.** Given the long tradition of Christians pursuing the common good, why do you think the church's reputation relative to the common good is what it is?

# Who Is Best Suited to Solve Community Problems?

*% ranked this option #1*

- 🔵 PRACTICING CHRISTIANS
- ⚪ NON-PRACTICING CHRISTIANS
- ⚫ NON-CHRISTIANS

31% 46% 42%
**Government**

33% 17% 7%
**Churches and Christian organizations**

18% 29% 26%
**Community members**

9% 13% 10%
**Charities**

7% 10% 9%
**Businesses**

2% 2% 3%
**Other religious organizations**

*n*=2,500 U.S. adults, July 25–August 15, 2019.

**FIGURE 1.3**

> **3.** What do you think the church and Christians are most known for if not for pursuing the common good?

Our current reputation would suggest that somewhere along the line we Christians have forgotten that we are created and called to pursue the common good. It turns out this is not new. From time to time God's people need to be reminded of their call to pursue the common good. And God, in his mercy, does just that.

## GRACIOUSLY REMINDED TO PURSUE THE COMMON GOOD

Let's consider a real-life example from early on in the life of the church: the Christians living in Asia Minor (modern-day Turkey) in the AD 60s. These Christians needed to be reminded to pursue the common good, and so God led Peter to write them a letter that did just that.

Why exactly did they need this reminder? These Christians faced a growing hostility from their neighbors stemming from Emperor Nero's increasingly negative view of Christians. Some of these Christians were tempted to fight back against their neighbors; some were tempted to withdraw from their neighbors; others were probably tempted to hide their faith and blend in with their neighbors. And all these temptations, while understandable, had the potential to pull their attention away from standing shoulder to shoulder with their neighbors to pursue the common good.

And so God led Peter to write them a letter that, among other things, reminded them of their call to pursue the common good. Consider this powerful line from Peter's letter: "Who is going to harm you if you are eager to do good?" (1 Peter 3:13 NIV).

This call to be "eager to do good" is a strong reminder to return to their God-given call to pursue the common good. Literally, Peter's words here remind the Christians in Asia Minor to "become zealous for making good things." The implication: they had, somewhere along the line, lost their zeal to do this.

Peter was clear that there was nothing new about this call, quoting from Psalm 34, a familiar psalm that called the Israelites to "do good" and "seek and pursue" shalom. In this way Peter graciously reminds the Christians in Asia Minor to not lose sight of what they are created for and called to do. While this reminder makes complete sense in light of Scripture, it could not have been simple or easy to hear in the midst of the increasing hostility they were experiencing. Given the fact that we may face our own tough seasons, let's try to imagine how this reminder might have landed on the ears of the original recipients of the letter. What might it have been like to be enduring persecution and then be reminded to pursue the common good?

## Pursuing the Common Good in Asia Minor

ANCYRA, GALATIA
SPRING, AD 62

*I am Tabitha and this is my city, the great hilltop city of Ancyra. We sit at the crossroads of the world, at the intersection of the flowing Ancyra Cayi and two well-used Roman highways. This is my home. But I've been daydreaming of gathering my household and leaving this place.*

*It's not that I don't love Ancyra. I do. How many mornings have I watched the sun rise in the east over my Galatian homeland? As the sun rises, I'm thankful for the God of Israel. I'm thankful for the gift of life. I am thankful for the comforts and traditions of our synagogue, for the health of all five of my children, and their children after them.*

*But these days my morning gaze looks not east at the rising sun but south at the rim of Cankaya—that distant hill to the south where the wealthy retreat in the heat of the summer. I long to go to Cankaya not to escape the heat of the summer but to escape the tension my family has felt ever since news of the Messiah came to Galatia.*

*The Pharisee Paul of Tarsus came into Galatia with the news of the Messiah. This news seemed to me to be straight from the mouth of the God of Israel. Paul's words rose over* me like the rising sun in the east, with a weight and authority surpassing anything I have heard in the synagogue.

Over time a strong, freeing faith in the Messiah grew within me and all my family. This change in us Christians—both Jews and, yes, even pagans—brings glory to God.

But this also brings shunning from the synagogue leaders, from all those in Ancyra who reject this humble Messiah. They look at our family differently now. This is because we sit with pagans at prayer and at table. We are seen as unclean. I never would have guessed my own children and their children after them would ever be looked at as unclean.

It makes me want to gather them all and fly away to Cankaya.

But this is not all that is in my heart. My daydreams have been interrupted by apostle Peter's letter. The letter arrived from Pontus only a few days ago. There is much in the letter to hold onto and remember, but one sentence in particular has made its way into my heart: "Who is going to harm you if you are eager to do good?"

Apostle Peter's meaning is simple enough: become zealous for shalom. However, the implications are anything but simple. The rabbis at the synagogue have taught us all about shalom: a flourishing of the people, peace at the border, good work in the market, kindness in the streets, food within houses.

But to become zealous for that? To pursue the welfare of Ancyra means staying here in Ancyra. It means standing with my neighbors contemplating the well-being of our borders and markets and streets and homes, not contemplating a flight to distant Cankaya.

Peter's words have invaded my daydreams and my heart, you see. Without even trying, I find my daydreams gravitating toward this hilltop under my feet, not distant, safe Cankaya. I wonder how we could help widow Aliah deal with her grief and adjust to life without her husband. I wonder how we can ease the burdens of the many travelers who use our roads. I wonder who could help repair the roof of the synagogue after the last storm.

Peter's words have done this to me; they have shifted my daydreams. I am left intrigued, confused, uncertain, excited. As I watch the sun rise in the east, I am thankful for the God of Israel and his humble Messiah. I watch the sun rise and its rays fill every street and corner and marketplace and house in Ancyra with God's warmth and light, and I think of Peter's words.

I feel the rising sun on my face and wonder, Can God bring true shalom to this hilltop?

1. If you were facing growing hostility from your neighbors, would you be more tempted to fight back, withdraw from them, or try to blend in with them?

2. Peter's reminder to be zealous to do good makes Tabitha feel "intrigued, confused, uncertain, excited." Which of these emotions makes the most sense to you? Which makes the least sense?

3. Have you ever found yourself daydreaming hopeful dreams about the common good of your neighborhood? What might help our thoughts go in that direction more naturally?

While we can only imagine what it would be like to be one of the original recipients of Peter's letter, we *can* unpack his clear reminder: even Christians living through a hostile season are called to stand with their neighbors and *become zealous for the common good.*

Peter put it in an interesting way in the original Greek: *to become zealous.* Zeal is a particular thing—it is the state of having such a strong emotion that we are compelled to action. This clarifies that Peter was not calling suffering Christians like Tabitha to *dutifully* partner with their neighbors. That would simply be a matter of the will. Peter is calling them to *become zealous* about this ancient shared human work.

This is pretty much the same call God gave the Israelites when they were brought to exile in Babylon. Recall that once in exile the Israelites were tempted to dream only of a quick escape. And so God had Jeremiah write them a letter (not unlike Peter's) to remind them of their call to pursue the common good right where they were. Jeremiah wrote, "Seek the welfare of the city where I have sent you into exile, and pray to the LORD on its behalf, for in its welfare you will find your welfare" (Jeremiah 29:7).

The word Jeremiah uses that is here translated "welfare" is *shalom*. The Israelites needed to be reminded to pursue the common good of the place God had brought them rather than dream of escaping that place. And history tells us that they did just that.

## PURSUING THE COMMON GOOD TODAY

And for us today? Whether we're in touch with the peacemaker wiring inside us or are more tempted to fight or flight or blend in, God's Word is alive today reminding us of our shared human work, inviting us to intertwine our hearts in the well-being of our community.

This is what the original concept of a *church parish* is all about. A parish is the local community surrounding the church and everyone and everything in it: Christians, non-Christians, stores, organizations, schools, trees, parks, farms, and so on. Similar to Berry's concept of "the membership," *parish* is a word that "recalls a geography large enough to live life together (live, work, play, etc.) and small enough to be known as a character within it."[17] This concept has helped Christians understand how interconnected all the pieces within a community are and the importance of pursuing the common good there.[18]

Jesus' call to be peacemakers, along with Peter and Jeremiah's letters, reminds us today that we too are to seek the welfare of the *parish* God has sent us into, expressing our faith in public through surprising (and maybe even sacrificial) acts of shalom.[19]

This is exactly what we see with Greg Russinger and his friends.

## Laundry Love

In 2003 Greg and some of his friends from church were zealous to pursue the common good of their community, Ventura, California. Instead of coming up

VENTURA,
CALIFORNIA
2003

with their own ideas of how to do this, they started by listening to their neighbors. One day they were talking to a neighbor who happened to be homeless and asked him, "What would it look like for us to come alongside your life?"

The man's response was simple and honest, "If I had clean clothes, I think people would treat me as a human being."

That comment sparked the peacemaker instinct inside Greg and his friends. *We can help our neighbor clean his clothes*, they thought. They knew that even clean clothes are a part of shalom. So they got some detergent and some quarters and helped their neighbor clean his clothes. Word got out, and they began helping other people clean their clothes too.

Their initial efforts at simple peacemaking sparked the peacemaker instincts inside other people and thus Laundry Love was born. Today the Laundry Love movement has spread to hundreds of locations across the country.

What's it all about? "Laundry Love washes the clothes and bedding of low/no income families and person(s) across the US. We brighten the lives of thousands of people through love, dignity, and detergent by partnering with diverse groups and laundromats nationwide."[a]

Greg and his friends (and now hundreds of people across the United States) are simply doing what Jeremiah and Peter remind us we are created and called to do: to pursue the common good of the place and people around us. They are making peace in their neighborhood.

1. Greg and his friends started by listening to lots of people in their community. What are the potential costs and benefits of such an approach?

2. In what different ways can helping clean clothes promote the common good of a neighborhood?

3. Why do you think Laundry Love has spread so quickly across the United States?

---

[a]Home page of Laundry Love, www.laundrylove.org.

Clearly, God nurtured within Greg and his friends real zeal for their community, Ventura. The latest research confirms that there is something important about having a zeal or passion for the well-being of those around us. When researchers asked people who were participants in a community of action why they were pursuing the common good, they discovered a wide variety of motivations: some more internal (focused on potential benefits to themselves and their group) and some more external (focused on potential benefits to the community).

And while internal motivations are more common on average,[20] researchers found that external motivations correspond to deeper engagement and more positive outcomes on the whole (see fig. 1.4.) Apparently, there is indeed something significant about what Peter called *becoming zealous* for the common good.

> **1.** Why do you think internal motivations are, on average, more common than external ones?
>
> **2.** What are some possible reasons that external motivations are stronger than internal ones?
>
> **3.** In reflecting on past times you have given time to making a difference, would you say your main motivations were external or internal?

These findings remind us of the good news we started with: all humans have been created to pursue the common good. It's what we're made for—whether it's accomplished through a good lunch, a warm greeting, an apt name, a welcoming household, a moment of forgiveness, a new business, a good day's work, a clean load of laundry, or reading books after school with a girl from the next apartment over. My first-grade teacher, Mrs. Love, was right: *we're all in this together.*

# The Power of Passion

**62%** of practicing Christians who participated in a community group shared a strong passion for the cause with their fellow group members. In several dimensions, this mutual enthusiasm correlates with deeper engagement and positive outcomes.

● COMMUNITY PARTICIPANTS IN GROUPS THAT SHARE A PASSION

○ COMMUNITY PARTICIPANTS IN GROUPS THAT DO NOT SHARE A PASSION

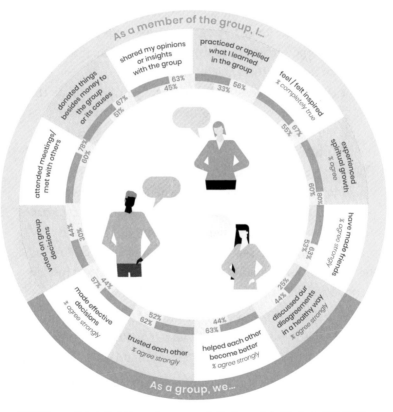

*As a member of the group, I...*

- shared my opinions or insights with the group — 63% / 45%
- practiced or applied what I learned in the group — 56% / 33%
- feel / felt inspired *% completely true* — 67% / 55%
- experienced spiritual growth *% agree* — 80% / 60%
- have made friends *% agree strongly* — 63% / 53%

*As a group, we...*

- donated things besides money to the group or its causes — 67% / 51%
- attended meetings / met with others — 78% / 60%
- voted on group decisions — 44% / 30%
- made effective decisions *% agree strongly* — 57% / 44%
- trusted each other *% agree strongly* — 52% / 62%
- helped each other become better *% agree strongly* — 44% / 63%
- discussed our disagreements in a healthy way *% agree strongly* — 25% / 44%

*n*=392 U.S. practicing Christians who were part of a group, July 25–August 19, 2019. Participants were asked to think about the most successful group they'd been a part of.

**FIGURE 1.4**

This shared work is not simple, of course. We need to be realistic: neighborhoods (and neighbors) are notoriously complex things in this fallen world, as I learned in a tragic way back in first grade. In this fallen world, it turns out, pursuing the common good is not for the faint of heart.

Today there are hints that the time is ripe for us to revisit and reclaim this powerful shared work. What a perfect time in our history to return to this ancient path.

But is that even possible? How exactly do we pursue the common good in our neighborhood? God's Word suggests a simple but revolutionary approach, and that's what we turn our thoughts to next.

Before we do, can you imagine it? Can you picture what it would look like if Christians everywhere shook off whatever temptations most distracted their thoughts and started daydreaming shalom for their neighborhoods? Just imagine . . .

What if we went against the flow of culture around us (fighting off the temptation to isolate and consume) and instead reconnected with our neighborhoods?

- Start right now by walking (or driving) around your neighborhood and reacquaint yourself with everything involved in "the membership" right around you.

- If you don't know any of your neighbors, try to meet a few of them this week.

- If you do know some neighbors, try to reconnect with them this week.

What if our current daydreams (of escape, of recreation, of vacation, of politics) became invaded by thoughts and visions and imagination of human flourishing?

- Get a map and draw a circle around what you would consider your neighborhood (some people suggest a quarter-mile to one-mile radius).

- Do some research about your neighborhood either at your library, online, or by asking some long-term residents of the neighborhood.

- Start a shalom journal, recording eight different dreams for your neighborhood.

What if the wideness and beauty and challenge of a big shalom vision got under our skin?

- Add a neighborhood section to whatever prayer rhythm you have—interceding for your neighborhood with all the other items you pray for.

- When you pray the Lord's Prayer, say (or think) your neighborhood's name when you pray "your will be done on earth as it is in heaven." For example, I could pray "your will be done in Pierremont as it is in heaven." If you aren't in the habit of praying the Lord's Prayer—try starting this practice. (See Matthew 6:5-15.)

■ Write "Pierremont Shalom" on a couple of sticky notes (inserting your own neighborhood, of course) and leave them in a couple of places where you are sure to see them during your day. See the difference it makes to have your thoughts triggered—even for a moment—back to what you wrote in your journal.

# 2

## Use Every Gift

**THE PROCESS OF BLESSING
YOUR NEIGHBORHOOD**

*Every good gift and every perfect
gift is from above, coming down
from the Father of lights.*

**JAMES 1:17**

I was living in rural Knox County, Tennessee, when I experienced the magic of resourcefulness for the first time. It was the summer before my third-grade year and my brother, Freddie, and I had accidentally started a forest fire.

We were spending a hot summer afternoon trimming the bushes around the rural house our family was renting. We were burning the trimmings in the burn barrel on the back of the property, between the potato garden and the woods. We were enjoying throwing more and more branches on the fire to really get it going and eventually (it's not too surprising looking back) the fire spread to the dry grass around the barrel and started advancing in a widening half circle toward the woods and all the dry underbrush that was waiting there.

When we realized we couldn't stomp out the fire, we ran and got Mom, who wisely got the water hose, but it only reached halfway to the burn barrel. So, Mom instructed us to bring a bucket and towels to the end of the hose. We filled the bucket, dipped the towels in and tried beating out the fire with the wet towels. It was a great idea, but by this point the half-circle was well into the woods and the fire seemed beyond our efforts. So, we retreated into the house to call the fire department.

And that's when it happened. My mom was on the phone in the kitchen (finding out it would take some time for the fire trucks to get to us—we lived in a pretty rural location) and my brother and I were standing close to Mom, feeling guilty and scared. I'm not sure what internal switch got flipped at that point (was it the guilt or fear or something else?) but all of a sudden I didn't want to wait. It felt wrong to just wait. It felt wrong to ignore the fire. And so I snuck out of the house and made my way back to the burn barrel.

I looked at the half circle of fire that had grown even bigger while we were inside. I looked around at what we had: a short hose, a bucket of water, and wet towels. I grabbed a heavy towel, went to the nearest side of the fire, and just started using that wet towel for all it was worth.

I don't remember many details from there, not until the fire trucks drove up the drive in a rush of noise and urgency. I was breathing hard at that point, gripping that near-ruined towel with both hands. And the fire was out. I remember the fire chief coming up to me with wide eyes and asking, "Are you the one that put the fire out?" Later, I would see my face in the bathroom mirror and realize my soot-smeared face had given me away.

But standing there gripping that towel, looking at the woods that I had (in my third-grade mind) just saved from certain annihilation, I felt the magic of making use of what I had at hand. That moment gave me a sense, even in third grade, that I was made to use the gifts God had put around me. It just felt right.

Of course, as I grew older I would feel the temptation to sit back and wait for the cavalry. There are usually plenty of people ready to swoop in and save the day, which can make me less attentive to the tools and resources already at hand. But when I eventually got around to studying what the Bible has to say about God's gift-giving, I discovered I had been right back in third grade. God entrusts all sorts of gifts to us so we can use them.

## BEAUTIFULLY CREATED TO USE EVERY GIFT

Let's consider another verse that mentions the shared work entrusted to humanity by their Creator: "God said to them, 'Be fruitful and multiply and fill the earth and subdue it, and have dominion over the fish of the sea and over the birds of the heavens and over every living thing that moves on the earth'" (Genesis 1:28).

The specific Hebrew verbs in this verse (*subdue* and *have dominion*) remind us, again, of the importance and weight of this mandate, clarifying that this work would require "energy of strength and the art of wisdom"[1] and "compassion" rather than a flippant posture of exploitation.[2] Right before this call to pursue the common good there's a short sentence that is long in implications: "God blessed them" (Genesis 1:28).

God blessed them. This is a powerful action communicated with a powerful Hebrew word, *barak*, which means to "bestow power for success, prosperity, fertility."[3] God isn't just wishing humans well (how we tend to think of "blessing"), rather he's actually bestowing on them power for success.

God charges humans with this mission to be fruitful and multiply only after he bestows on them the power to accomplish that mission. God doesn't just make humans his partners in crafting shalom, but he also bestows on them what they need to do that crafting. This means that people of every creed and no creed have talents and abilities and knowledge and resources given to them by their gracious Creator for the pursuit of peacemaking.[4]

As Christians, when we think of gifts we sometimes think specifically of the spiritual gifts that the Holy Spirit entrusts to Christians. But God also graciously gives gifts (we might call them "common gifts") to every human he creates. At the very beginning of creation God exhibited and exercised his gift-giving nature with all of humanity. We read in the very next words in Genesis 1: "God said, 'Behold, *I have given you* every plant yielding seed that is on the face of all the earth, and every tree with seed in its fruit. You shall have them for 'food'" (Genesis 1:29 emphasis added).

We shouldn't rush by this gift-giving. In fact, notice how God invites us to pause and pay attention: "*Behold*, I have given you ..." Saying *behold* is the equivalent of saying, "Pay attention to this! Look!" This is an invitation to pay attention to the good gifts he gives us. This would include the gift of the people God places around us. Consider a specific example we have of this early in Genesis: "Then the LORD God said, 'It is not good that the man should be alone; I will make him a helper fit for him'" (Genesis 2:18).

This is a very tender, attentive bit of gift-giving. In this phrase "a helper fit for him" God reveals an intimate knowledge of what Adam needs. Adam needs a helper—pursuing shalom is not a solo job. And Adam needs a helper "fit for him"—literally the Hebrew here means "according to the opposite of him" and could be taken as meaning "corresponding" to him.[5] This is a tailor-made gift if you will. God knows that to pursue the common good Adam will need someone who is like him but also different from him, his "fitting complement."[6]

This is an important moment. It's not just a great example of God's gift-giving, it also shows us that among the gifts God gives to humans are other humans. People are gifts. We need people who are differently shaped and differently gifted from us. We are gifts to each other, designed to stand shoulder to shoulder as we engage in our shared work.

This isn't just for Israelites or Christians, of course. Just as God causes the rain to fall and the sun to shine on all people everywhere (Matthew 5:45), so God distributes good gifts to all people everywhere. As we see in James, "every good gift and every perfect gift" is given to us by God (James 1:17). This is true whether the gift is a Christian friend, a non-Christian neighbor, a physical skill, an intellectual aptitude, a creative flair, or material blessings of many kinds—every good gift is from God. God gives these gifts out of his "divine goodness and mercy" not through any merit on the part of we humans.[7] Even non-Christians who may not recognize where their gifts come from are gifted by God and given to the place and people around them, their neighborhood, as a gift. God's gifts are spread abundantly among the just and unjust in ways that support and enhance the lives of all.[8]

We were created to pursue the common good, yes. But before diving into this exciting task, God invites us to pause and *behold* the gifts he has placed in us and all around us. Those gifts are what we need to successfully pursue the common good.

## Paradigm Shift
### FROM SCARCITY TO ABUNDANCE

There is a paradigm shift going on in the realm of forestry. For years there had been a consensus among ecologists that all trees were independent operators, each tree an island unto itself, the forest a place of limited, scarce resources where trees competed with each other. Trees were seen as "disconnected loners, competing for water, nutrients and sunlight, with the winners shading out the losers and sucking them dry."[a]

But that's beginning to change. When ecologist Suzanne Simard discovered underground connectivity between trees in her field experiments, scientists began to see the forest through new eyes. Scientists like Simard and German forester Peter Wohlleben began to study the many ways trees are connected through underground fungal networks and *share* resources with each other. If we could pull back the forest floor, we would actually see white and yellow threads crisscrossed and going off in multiple directions connecting each tree with an abundance of resources embedded in its neighbor trees throughout the forest.[b]

Given what we read in Genesis 1 about God's gift-giving, perhaps it's time for Christians to undergo a similar paradigm shift in how we see our neighborhoods. For years there has been a tendency to view our neighborhoods (especially historically struggling places) through a skeptical lens: we notice problems first, and we assume resources are scarce in a community. Thus we're tempted to ride in with truckloads of resources to save the struggling community. The usual service experience starts by looking for problems.

But what if that changed? What if we became (at least) as interested in the gifts God is entrusting to the people and neighborhood as we were in the apparent problems of a neighborhood? What if we followed the lead of Genesis (and the confirmed insights of community development experts) and paused to *behold* the gifts in us and around us, and took our cues for pursuing the common good from that abundance?[c] What if we assumed God has already given us and our neighbors an abundance of gifts rather than a scarcity of gifts?

1. How does it feel to learn that trees are connected through vast underground networks of fungi and share resources with each other?

2. In what ways are neighborhoods like an interconnected forest? In what ways are they different?

3. What are some of the differences you think it might make to behold what is strong in a community before discerning how to address what seems wrong?

[a]Richard Grant, "Do Trees Talk to Each Other?" *Smithsonian*, March 2018, www.smithsonianmag.com/science-nature/the-whispering-trees -180968084.

[b]Suzanne Simard, "How Do Trees Collaborate?," Ted Radio Hour (January 13, 2017), National Public Radio.

[c]See John P. Kretzmann and John L. McKnight, *Building Communities from the Inside Out: A Path Toward Finding and Mobilizing a Community's Assets* (Chicago: ACTA Publications, 1993).

## EXPLICITLY CALLED TO USE EVERY GIFT

Every human is blessed and entrusted with gifts, but at our fall into sin, our clarity about that blessing and those gifts got shaken and cracked along with everything else. And so God began to explicitly *call* humans to notice and use the gifts he was giving them.

Throughout history God keeps having to say "Behold" to remind people that he blesses them and entrusts them with gifts. For example, when the Israelites grew inattentive to God's blessed presence, he sent the prophets to call the people to avail themselves of God's presence through prayer and worship. When the people grew inattentive to God's law (literally misplacing the law for years!) God had King Josiah call the people to avail themselves of the gift of the law.

We see a memorable echo of this call to avail ourselves of the gifts God entrusts to us in Jesus' parable of the talents. The faithful servants are those who used the money (gifts) entrusted to them by their master to do business, and the unfaithful servant simply buried what his master had given him. Jesus is inviting his disciples to *behold* the many gifts God has entrusted into their hands.

And when we read the rest of the New Testament, it appears that's exactly what they did. The early church was alive with the use of gifts. Whether those gifts were money (Acts 2:43-47), land (Acts 4:32-37), spiritual gifts (Acts 6:8), leadership abilities (Acts 15:1-21), visions (Acts 10), other people (Acts 6:1-7), or the greatest gift of all—the gospel of Jesus (Acts 2:14-36), the early church responded to Jesus' call to use every gift God had given them.

## Using Every Gift Throughout History

Even when the early disciples *seemed* to have very little (an apparent scarcity of gifts), their eyes were open to *behold* the ample gifts God was putting all around them. Consider a striking example from the first few generations of Christians.

During the first centuries of the Christian church, at least two major epidemics swept through the Roman Empire, decimating up to a full third of the population of the empire.[a] So devastating were these diseases that throughout the Roman Empire people "crouched in fear" when the first indications of one of the diseases came to their region.[b] As Thucydides had written centuries before, the only sensible thing to do when a disease was spreading was flee.[c] And, indeed, when the disease first hit a town people "became indifferent to every rule of religion or law" and fled, leaving the sick to die where they lay.[d]

Christians responded differently. History tells us that Jesus' followers were so zealous for the common good that they stayed behind to care for the sick. In fact, in many cases the only functioning social network remaining after a disease hit a neighborhood was the church.[e]

While an objective observer may have concluded that these heroic Christians had a *scarcity* of resources to use (they had no cure for the disease), Christians looked at what gifts they did have (an *abundant* ability to comfort and clean and feed the sick) and used those. Christians stayed in the neighborhood and compassionately administered nursing and care for those who were sick. This was both inspiring and tragic. Dionysius wrote about Christians around AD 260 during the height of the second great epidemic: "Heedless of danger, they took charge of the sick, attending to their every need and ministering to them in Christ, and with them departed this life serenely happy; for they were infected by others with the disease, drawing on themselves the sickness of their neighbors and cheerfully accepting their pains."[f]

Not only were these efforts inspiring and tragic, but they were also, in the end, fruitful. As it turns out, the conscientious nursing from Christians provided just enough physical relief and wholesome sustenance that mortality rates were *curbed* by the Christians' loving presence.[g]

1. What are the various ways people are tempted to respond to new epidemics? How are you tempted to respond?

2. What did Christians risk by staying to care for the sick? What must that time have been like as towns emptied out of all but the sick and the Christians?

3. Make a list of the gifts the remaining Christians did *not* have and a list of the gifts they did have. How do these lists compare? Would you say they had a scarcity or abundance of gifts? Why?

---

[a]Rodney Stark, *The Rise of Christianity: How the Obscure, Marginal Jesus Movement Became the Dominant Religious Force in the Western World in a Few Centuries* (Princeton, NJ: Princeton University Press, 1996), 73.

[b]Stark, *Rise of Christianity*, 74.

[c]Stark, *Rise of Christianity*, 85.

[d]Stark, *Rise of Christianity*, 85.

[e]Andy Crouch, *Culture Making: Recovering Our Creative Calling* (Downers Grove, IL: InterVarsity Press, 2008), 156-57.

[f]Stark, *Rise of Christianity*, 82.

[g]Stark, *Rise of Christianity*, 88-89.

The heroic Christian response to the devastating epidemics in the Roman Empire is inspiring. But Christians can forget from time to time that they are created and called to use every gift in such heroic ways. And so we need to be reminded to *behold* every gift God has given us. And God, in his mercy, does just that.

## GRACIOUSLY REMINDED TO USE EVERY GIFT

In the same letter Peter wrote to remind the Christians in Asia Minor to pursue the common good, he also reminded them to use every gift in that pursuit of that common good: "As each has received a gift, use it to serve one another, as good stewards of God's varied grace" (1 Peter 4:10).

Why do they need to be reminded to use every gift in pursuing the common good? Tough seasons have a way of making us curl in on ourselves—selfishness and a narrowing of vision are common temptations when life is difficult. Peter invites Christians in Asia Minor to lift their heads up from their troubles and become attentive again to the gifts God has given and is giving them. He invites them to repent of their understandable scarcity mindset and return to their God-given abundance of gifts. Think of the strategy this implies.

Rather than invite Christians to pursue the common good in any random way, Peter wants them to pause first and *behold* the gifts God has given them. Rather than rush ahead with the first idea about peacemaking that pops into their heads (possibly with a scarcity mindset in their heart), Peter invites them to be attentive to the gifts God has already placed in them, in their neighbors, and throughout their neighborhood.

This may seem simple enough as a strategy, but it is revolutionary and powerful. Given how we sometimes forget to *behold* or use every gift God has given us, let's try to imagine how these words might have landed on the ears of the original recipients of the letter. Exactly how revolutionary and practical is this reminder to pay attention to gifts?

# Using Every Gift in Asia Minor

SMYRNA,
ASIA
FALL, AD 62

*I feel like a new man with new eyes. I'm not new at all, of course. Myrina and I have seen five full decades each! We are growing older here in this port town beside the mighty Aegean. But as I walk these familiar streets I am seeing them and all they hold as if for the first time.*

*I am Strabo. And this is my city, Smyrna. If you visit our busy port or inspect the Roman garrison or start up the inland passages, you will be walking on roads my own two hands helped build. These are strong Roman roads.*

*I've grown strong building these wide stone-paved roads. As a mason I select and shape and place the stones. So they fit just right. I calculate angles, so each stretch of road is cambered for drainage. I make sure the bridleways and footpaths are solid.*

*This takes a good eye. And I've always thought I had a good one. My team is still praised for our work on the Golden Road. It takes a good eye to lay a central road like that, angled to follow the lie of the hill. I always thought I had a good eye—until hearing that new letter from Peter.*

*Peter's letter was brought here from Cappadocia nearly six weeks ago. There was much in the letter for new Christ* followers to hear and put thought to. Much I am still thinking and praying about. But there was one sentence that haunts me and has changed my eyes: "As each has received a gift, use it to serve one another" (1 Peter 4:10).

The words are simple in meaning. But they are changing my eyes. I have lived in Smyrna these five decades. My mason's eyes have noticed more details than most, I imagine. But I feel like I am seeing my Smyrna for the first time.

I see gifts everywhere I look.

My eyes are trained to survey the countryside for useful stones. Now my eye surveys Smyrna, and I see gifts everywhere I look. The gifts of bird and bush, rain and sun. But also the gifts of neighbor and friend, talent and passion.

Realizing we are called to use all these gifts to build roads of shalom fills me with the excitement of a young apprentice. What a great building project this is!

Every person I run into (I've known them my whole life!) I now see as a gift from God. Even Himerius, my elderly neighbor I usually try to avoid, I see he is a gift given to me and to all of Smyrna. His patient ear and slow tongue I've always seen as a distraction. But I see now he is a gift to the lonely and the road weary.

Myrina often teases me that I am more interested in the stones underneath my feet than the people standing in front of me. And she is right. But even Myrina has noticed a difference in me. I wonder, Has God called me to a holy building project? Not a Golden Road this time but a golden good?

*To partner with God in his work of bringing shalom is a high calling. Building roads of goodness here in Smyrna is the highest honor I can imagine. This thought keeps me up at night. I feel dignity unlike any I have ever felt. And I see dignity in all my neighbors with their many God-given gifts. It keeps me up at night as I wonder what we should build first.*

1. Strabo claims that Peter's letter has given him "new eyes." Compare and contrast how Strabo used to see and how he sees now.

2. Peter uses a builder's term when inviting Christians in Asia Minor to pursue the common good. What are some of the similarities and differences that Strabo notices between building Roman roads and building the common good?

3. What do you tend to notice the most as you spend time in or travel around your neighborhood?

In the midst of Peter's exciting reminder to pursue the common good comes an equally important reminder to use every gift. Rather than simply rush ahead with their ideas of how to pursue the common good, Peter encourages them to stop and first pay attention to the gifts God has already placed around them.

## USING EVERY GIFT TODAY

Paying attention to gifts turns out to be a revolutionary and powerful way of pursuing the common good. It is not uncommon for our pursuit of the common good to begin with problems instead. We see a problem and we try to do something about it. When we start with problems in this way, the basic contours of pursuing the common good look like this:

1. Identify a problem.

2. Come up with a solution.

3. Implement the solution.

While this simple three-step process works in simpler matters, it can become problematic when working toward the common good of an actual neighborhood. By starting with problems, we often overlook the abundant gifts and complex realities of the neighborhood itself, which is why experts in community development have sounded an alarm about the many potential dangers of this approach.[9]

Peter's reminder to use every gift points to a refreshing way to pursue the common good. Rather than starting with problems (and a mindset of scarcity), we start where God wants us to start: *beholding* what gifts he has given us and our neighbors. We start by recognizing that every human is a gift from God and is blessed with gifts. We treat people as if they have gifts and are waiting to offer them.[10]

Strabo was right to be excited by this reminder. And we should be too. In essence, we're invited to a much different three-step process:

1. Discover the gifts.

2. Imagine the possibilities.

3. Pursue the common good.

This is a powerful, biblical process that we can still follow today. By starting with gifts, we take God's lead. We recognize that God is the giver of gifts, and it is our role to steward those gifts, as Peter put it. Sounds simple enough. But the genius of Peter's method is that it avoids the potential pitfalls of "white knighting" and comports with best practices social scientists point to for those wanting to pursue the common good.[11] The formal term among community developers is "asset-based community development," but it's really all about what Peter reminds us to do: start with the gifts and move out from there. Behold the gifts and *then* pursue the common good.

In this way we begin to see the neighborhood as a treasure chest.[12] We can pursue the common good by curiously discovering the gifts God has given us, creatively imagining the possibilities those gifts point to, and then collaboratively pursuing the common good.

## The Hopeful Neighborhood Project's Three-Step Process

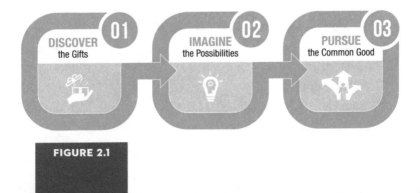

**FIGURE 2.1**

We can do this with any of our neighbors, whether they are Christian or not. All people in our neighborhoods are a gift from God with gifts to share—even those neighbors we may be tempted to look right over or dismiss.

To find out more about how you and your neighbors can do this three-step process together, check out the various online tools available through the Hopeful Neighborhood Project (hopefulneighborhood.org) to help you along this three-step process, which you can see in figure 2.1.

These practical tools (including *The Hopeful Neighborhood Field Guide: Six Lessons on Pursuing the Common Good Right Where You Live*[13]) are designed by the Hopeful Neighborhood Project to help small groups of neighbors (Christian or not) stand shoulder to shoulder and pursue the common good of their neighborhood together.

> Vocation: "all the different roles God has called you into, including roles in family, society, workplace, and (for Christians) the church—through which you serve your neighbors, the actual human beings God has placed in your life."[14]

The fact that our shared work requires the use of all the gifts God has blessed us with should cause us to appreciate and celebrate, among other things, the reality of vocation. It is good that God has gifted each of us differently and called each of us

## What, If Anything, Does Your Community Need That Churches or Christian Organizations Could Provide?

● PRACTICING CHRISTIANS  ○ NON-CHRISTIANS

| | Practicing Christians | Non-Christians |
|---|---|---|
| Homeless services | 62% | 42% |
| Youth or children's clubs / events | 57% | 24% |
| Counseling services | 56% | 22% |
| Companionship for the elderly | 55% | 30% |
| Support for single parents | 51% | 22% |
| Fundraising for charities | 47% | 25% |
| Substance abuse recovery support | 44% | 23% |
| Practical services in the community | 37% | 20% |
| Work in local schools | 35% | 12% |
| Refugee and immigrant services | 27% | 21% |
| Access to healthcare services | 27% | 16% |
| Prison or justice reform | 26% | 15% |
| Debt relief / financial advice | 26% | 15% |
| Sports programs | 22% | 8% |
| Advocacy / campaigning | 18% | 6% |
| I don't believe Christians / churches should provide any of these | 2% | 24% |
| None of these are needed | 2% | 3% |

*n*=1,505 U.S. practicing Christian adults and 264 non-Christian U.S. adults who were part of a group, July 25–August 15, 2019.

**FIGURE 2.2**

to different vocations. We can find God and his gifts "in the very fabric of our calling as teachers, as nurses, as engineers, as artists, and as writers."[15] It is often *through* our vocations (not despite them) that we can reflect the goodness of God and his designs for shalom and human flourishing.[16] Some of us are called to create beauty (creative careers), others to cultivate abundance (entrepreneurial careers), generate order (STEM careers), or directly care for those in need (service careers).[17] It is a thin view of shalom-building that would imply that only pastors or missionaries or Christians get to be involved in the great common-good project. This is a shared work because we are each so differently gifted.

The latest research confirms our neighborhoods' needs for all sorts of vocations. Researchers asked people what, if anything, their community needs that churches or Christian organizations could potentially provide. As you can see in figure 2.2, people identified a wide variety of tangible needs as possible places for Christians to make a difference in the community. Notice the wide variety of practical needs that would naturally call for a wide variety of gifts, skills, expertise, and resources to meet—requiring people with all different sorts of vocations.

It is also fascinating to notice the similarities (and differences!) when comparing this list in figure 2.2 with the list in figure 2.3 which shows the programs churches are currently offering.

# Programs Churches Offer

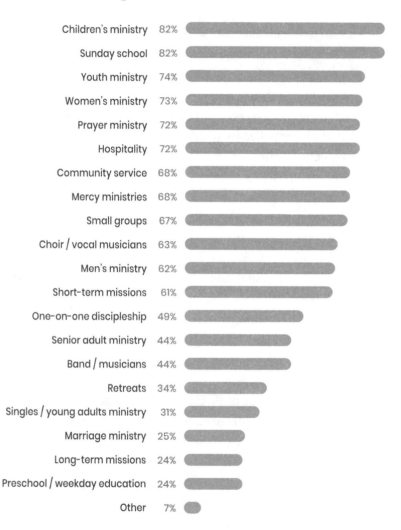

| Program | % |
|---|---|
| Children's ministry | 82% |
| Sunday school | 82% |
| Youth ministry | 74% |
| Women's ministry | 73% |
| Prayer ministry | 72% |
| Hospitality | 72% |
| Community service | 68% |
| Mercy ministries | 68% |
| Small groups | 67% |
| Choir / vocal musicians | 63% |
| Men's ministry | 62% |
| Short-term missions | 61% |
| One-on-one discipleship | 49% |
| Senior adult ministry | 44% |
| Band / musicians | 44% |
| Retreats | 34% |
| Singles / young adults ministry | 31% |
| Marriage ministry | 25% |
| Long-term missions | 24% |
| Preschool / weekday education | 24% |
| Other | 7% |

*n*=508 U.S. Protestant pastors, July 25–August 13, 2019.

**FIGURE 2.3**

**1.** Make a list of the different skills, resources, and abilities it would take to meet each of the needs listed in figure 2.2. How many items on your list would you say your neighbors possess, as far as you know?

**2.** Considering the top of the list, why do you think people are more open to Christians' help in those particular areas? Looking at the bottom of the list, why do you think fewer people are open to Christians' help in those areas?

**3.** What are the similarities and differences between figure 2.2 and figure 2.3? What might explain these similarities or differences?

Today we may not be in the business of making impressive Roman roads as Strabo of Smyrna, but this call from Peter's letter remains a call on all our lives. It is still today *blessed* to be a peacemaker and to use every gift. This is exactly what Rebekah Morris and her students have done and the results have changed their neighborhood.

## Las Vecinas De Buford Highway

In 2017 Rebekah Morris was teaching English and journalism at Cross Keys High School, a public high

ATLANTA, GEORGIA
2017

school in Atlanta. Noticing that her students had really important, insightful things to say about their community, Rebekah created a group assignment for her ninth-grade students to research and write about how to pursue the common good in their community.

Even though most of these students had only fifth- and sixth-grade reading levels, they wound up compiling a list of powerful insights, knowledge, and observations. They were, it turned out, experts on their own neighborhood. Because their neighborhood is mostly composed of a series of apartments along Buford Highway on the north side of Atlanta, many of their insights centered on how to promote the well-being of those living in the apartments.

The final class assignment was to present their ideas to the city council, mayor, community members, and stakeholders. And they did just that, presenting practical, wise ideas for improving affordable housing, pedestrian walkways, and more. Their ideas were so spot-on that their presentation drew the attention of the local press: these ninth graders made people rethink what gifts were already planted all along Buford Highway.

Rebekah and the students were so encouraged and empowered that they formed a club to keep the project going even after the class ended. Soon they were holding dinners in apartments to tap into the gifts and insights of those living in the various apartment complexes. Neighbors shared their wisdom, leadership gifts began to blossom, residents got more connected to local agencies and government offices. As tangible improvements to the neighborhood mounted, an association, Los Vecinos (The Neighbors), was born and is now active in more than twenty apartment complexes.

Rebekah and her students (and now hundreds of people living in their community) were simply doing what Genesis and Peter tell us we're created and called to do: use every gift that God has given us and our neighbors. By tapping into the gifts God had already placed in the neighborhood the common good along Buford Highway has improved.

1. Rebekah started by asking ninth-graders to use their knowledge and insights and relationships to pursue the well-being of their community. What are the potential costs and benefits of inviting younger people to use their God-given gifts?

2. In what different ways can encouraging those within a community to have a voice promote the common good of that community?

3. Why do you think the students wanted to keep their class assignment going? Why do you think their approach began spreading to other apartment complexes?

Our current season is perhaps uniquely suited for a return to this biblical call to use every gift to pursue the common good. As we've seen, ours is an age when trust for Christian organizations and churches and leaders is lower than it has been in some time. The modern era may have been an age of trusted Christian organizations, but the postmodern era may just turn out to be the age of the helpful Christian neighbor. Trust can be rebuilt as we stand shoulder to shoulder with our neighbors, bringing our gifts together to create "homegrown, homemade solutions."[18]

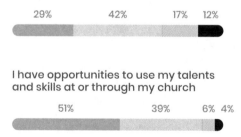

## Vocation & the Church
*Base: practicing Christian community participants*

● STRONGLY AGREE
○ SOMEWHAT AGREE
○ SOMEWHAT DISAGREE
● STRONGLY DISAGREE

**I wish I could better connect my vocation (profession or skills) to serving at or through my church**

| 29% | 42% | 17% | 12% |
|-----|-----|-----|-----|

**I have opportunities to use my talents and skills at or through my church**

| 51% | 39% | 6% | 4% |
|-----|-----|-----|-----|

*n*=392 U.S. practicing Christian adults who were part of a group, July 25–August 15, 2019.

**FIGURE 2.4**

The latest research indicates, however, that stopping to *behold* what gifts God has given us and the people around us is something we may need to pay closer attention to. As you can see in figure 2.4, only 51 percent of practicing Christians strongly agree that they have opportunities to use their unique talents and skills at or through their church.

A full 71 percent of practicing Christians either strongly agree or somewhat agree that they wish they could better connect their vocation to serving at or through their church. Perhaps, just like the Christians living in Asia Minor, we need a reminder to *behold* the many gifts God has entrusted us with that we can use to pursue the common good of our neighborhoods.

1. Using the scale given in figure 2.4, how much do you agree or disagree with each statement?

2. What people do you know who wish they could better connect their vocation (their profession and skills) with their serving? What do you think has kept them from making that connection already?

3. What are some ways you think churches could help people be more thoughtful about how to use their vocation in practical ways in the church or community?

When our neighbors are quick to dismiss Christian professionals and programs, what a perfect moment to rediscover

Peter's call to use our collective gifts to pursue the common good. When experts are concluding that association groups of volunteers can deliver a level of affection and care that is impossible for professionals or institutions, what a perfect season to partner with our neighbors (Christian or not) to engage in the shared work God designed us for.[19]

But what about this distrust Christians are sometimes facing in our country these days? When so many Christians feel defensive in our culture, is this really the time and place for joining with our non-Christian neighbors in pursuit of the common good?

God's Word gives us a refreshing and important answer to these understandable questions, and that's what we turn our thoughts to next.

But before we do, can you imagine it? Can you picture what it would look like if Christians everywhere became stewards of God-given gifts? Just imagine . . .

What if we curiously cataloged all the gifts we have and celebrated them not as things we happen to have but as *gifts* that are *entrusted* into our hands?

- Make a list of the different vocations God has called you to in this season of your life (remembering roles in family, society, workplace, and church).

- Ask a couple of close friends or family members what they think some of your natural gifts are.

- Go online right now to take a personal gift inventory available at hopefulneighborhood.org to get a better perspective on exactly what God has entrusted you with.

What if we saw the people around us (and all their cataloged gifts) not as people we happen to live near but as *gifts* that we and our neighborhood need?

- Make a list of the people in your life that you know are gifts to you. Spend time thanking God for those gifts.
- Make a list of people in your life who don't necessarily always feel like gifts. Ask God to reveal to you how they are gifts to you and your family or neighborhood or workplace or church.
- Write down the names of five neighbors right now who you want to forward the personal-gift assessment to so you can all learn about your gifts together.

What if we looked around at all the parks and bus stops and businesses and groups and loose associations and offices and buildings and roads of our neighborhoods not as so much stage dressing that happens to be there but as *gifts* that we get to *steward*?

- Go online right now to take a neighborhood gift inventory at hopefulneighborhood.org to begin the process of thinking in new ways about all the gifts God has already placed in your neighborhood.

- Ask one or two neighbors what they like most about your neighborhood.

- Spend time praying prayers of thanks to God for the specific gifts in your neighborhood (thanking him for parks, specific trees, favorite stores, level sidewalks, etc.).

# 3

## Love Everyone Always

### THE POWER OF GRACE IN TOUGH SEASONS

*You have heard that it was said, "You shall love your neighbor and hate your enemy." But I say to you, Love your enemies.*

**MATTHEW 5:43-44**

I was living in oil country in Odessa, Texas, the first time I experienced the power of responding to meanness with kindness. It was the first day of fifth grade, my first day at this new school in the desert of West Texas, and I was not having a great day.

For starters, it didn't help that I unknowingly brought my Appalachian appearance with me from the backwoods of Knox County, Tennessee: long hair, high-water jeans, drooping socks, and a twang that was unlike the West Texas accents that every other kid in the school had. The truth is, I didn't know I was poor until that first day going to school with oil industry kids clad in bright Izod and polo shirts, their collars confidently popped.

And then there's just the whole new kid dynamic. The day started by my teacher assigning me to Steve—the most popular kid in the whole class. He was to be my partner that week—showing me the ropes, helping me find the lunchroom, the library, and so on. Steve, I surmised by the look he gave me, was not happy about this assignment.

My suspicions were confirmed every time Steve had to interact with me. He frowned at me, spoke quickly, and otherwise ignored me. Every single time I responded to Steve's indifference with kindness. I smiled back at his frowns. I thanked him for his roughly-offered help. Make no mistake—this was no saintly posture on my part; it was sheer desperation. Steve was all I had, so I was nice to him. Things got more complicated, though, during my first physical education class.

The coach took all of us outside to the playground where we stood in a big circle under the hot desert sun. And that's where it happened. As I stood there with my drooping socks exposed by my too-short jeans, my long hair blowing in the wind, one of the boys pointed at me and said for all to hear, "Hey coach, is that guy a guy or a girl?" To his credit, the coach put a quick end to the laughter, but the damage was done. He-Man action dolls were a big thing at the time and so my nickname from that moment forward became She-Man.

And my response? Whether because of first-day desperation or a lack of creativity, I decided to beat their meanness with kindness.

And that's just what I did. Not with a subservient or weak acquiescence but with regular, sturdy kindness. I became friends with the boys in my physical education class; I became an active, vocal, upbeat presence in the classroom; and best of all Steve and I became friends. Best friends, in fact. Steve turned out to be an incredible human and friend, and we are still friends to this day.

That year in oil country I first felt the true power of responding to meanness with kindness. That year I was convinced, even as a young fifth grader, that I was made to respond to whatever life threw at me with kindness and love. It just felt right.

Of course, as I grew older I would feel the temptation to punch back, to grow bitter and angry. There are plenty of mean people and tough seasons in life, and so I tried my hand at frowns and grudges and even a couple of fistfights over the years. But when I eventually got around to studying what the Bible has to say about how God made all of us, I discovered that I had been right back in fifth grade. We are made to love everyone. And love, it turns out, is always powerful.

## BEAUTIFULLY CREATED TO LOVE EVERYONE ALWAYS

If we read the first sentence of the Bible, it is noteworthy that God himself, implicitly, preceded creation: "In the beginning,

God created the heavens and the earth" (Genesis 1:1). Before any creating happened there was just God. In the beginning, God. That was it. Bearing in mind John's reminder that "God is love" (1 John 4:8), we can surmise that before anything was created there was love. In the beginning there was God, who is love. As John reminds us, this then is where our call to love originates, "Beloved, let us love one another, for love is from God" (1 John 4:7).

> Love: "Love is patient, love is kind. It does not envy, it does not boast, it is not proud. It does not dishonor others, it is not self-seeking, it is not easily angered, it keeps no record of wrongs. Love does not delight in evil but rejoices with the truth. It always protects, always trusts, always hopes, always perseveres." (1 Corinthians 13:4-7 NIV)

In the beginning we were created for love. We see, for example, a genuine loving relationship between God and humans in the garden. Adam and Eve were "created to relate to God in a way that none of the other created beings" were.[1] One of the most tender descriptions of this comes to us from a passage describing the unfortunate first moments that loving relationship was cracked: "They heard the sound of the LORD God walking in the garden in the cool of the day, and the man and his wife hid themselves from the presence of the LORD God among the trees of the garden. But the LORD God called to the man and said to him, 'Where are you?'" (Genesis 3:8-9).

The tragedy of the scene is enhanced by how natural this loving relationship between God and humans was before their sin and subsequent hiding: they would go on walks together; they talked with each other. In the beginning humans were designed to be loved by God and to love him.

Humans were also created to love and be loved by each other. The fact that Adam's aloneness was deemed as "not good" (Genesis 2:18) is a reminder that humans are created to be social animals.[2] And God created all these social animals from one man (rather than impersonally stamping out disparate humans in a factory), perhaps "in order that our desire of mutual accord might be the greater, and that each might more freely embrace the other as his own flesh."[3]

The word *love* may not be written on the first page of the Bible, but it is shown. God was love, and his creation was infused by love. Humanity was created to love and be loved. This was true for Adam and Eve. And this is true for you and me and every single person you've ever loved or hated, talked to or ignored.

## Paradigm Shift
### FROM CONVERSATION TO DIATRIBE

A paradigm shift is happening in the realm of conversation. For centuries the art of conversation (a respectful, fruitful, sometimes messy give-and-take between people) has been celebrated and encouraged and honed. From ancient thinkers (think of Plato's *Symposium* or Cicero's *On Oratory*) to modern thinkers (there were fifty works on conversation published in Europe in the first half of the eighteenth century alone), we humans have nurtured and enjoyed healthy and enriching conversation between humans.[a] You could say that "face-to-face conversation is the most human—and humanizing—thing we do."[b] And the default conversation has been face-to-face and has involved listening, empathy, and respect—even in the presence of strong disagreements.

But that's beginning to change. Increasingly conversation is being eroded by anger and "an atmosphere of unrelenting contention" that has left conversation in bad shape in contemporary America.[c] Some believe this erosion of conversation is due to the advent of digital communication.[d] Others point to the various ways our popular culture is hostile to real conversation by encouraging excessive politeness (*Don't be judgmental*) and excessive impoliteness (*Express yourself*) all while implicitly endorsing anger.[e] Whatever the reason, ours is increasingly the age of "the screed, the rant, the tirade, the jeremiad, the diatribe, the venom-fueled, white-hot harangue!"[f] This shift from conversation to diatribe is well documented, as can be seen in the recent spate of books on just this topic.[g]

Given what we see in Genesis about humans being created for loving relationships, it would seem obvious that we Christians need to actively resist this paradigm shift. Regardless of the flow of culture around us, we have the first chapters of the Bible in our hands—chapters that show us that every single human we ever interact with or talk to or live by is made to love and to be loved. The paradigmatic human interaction for Christians ought to be colored by love.

What if we resisted this dehumanizing conversational trend going on around us? What if we infused listening, empathy, and respect into all of our conversations—digital or otherwise. What if we got honest with ourselves about the unique temptations that come with digital communication and pledged ourselves to behave in refreshingly graceful ways digitally?[h] What if we spurned diatribes and embraced gracious face-to-face conversations—even in the presence of strong disagreements?

1. What evidence have you personally seen, if any, that confirms our Western culture is moving away from conversation toward more diatribes?

2. How have you noticed yourself or others interacting differently in digital spaces (email, social media, texting, etc.)?

3. On a scale of 1 to 10, how loving would you say most of your interactions with others are during an average day? How do you feel about that number?

---

[a]Stephen Miller, *Conversation: A History of a Declining Art* (New Haven, CT: Yale University Press, 2006), 80.

[b]Sherry Turkle, *Reclaiming Conversation: The Power of Talk in a Digital Age* (New York: Penguin, 2015), 3.

cDeborah Tannen as quoted in Miller, *Conversation*, xii; and Miller, *Conversation*, xi.

dSee, for example, Sherry Turkle, *Reclaiming Conversation: The Power of Talk in a Digital Age* (New York: Penguin, 2015).

eMiller, *Conversation*, 296.

fPeter Carlson, "It's All the Rage," *Washington Post*, February 13, 2003.

gSee, for example, Deborah Tannen, *The Argument Culture* (New York: Random House, 1998); John L. Locke *The De-Voicing of Society: Why We Don't Talk To Each Other Anymore* (New York: Touchstone, 1998); William Eadie and Paul E. Nelson, eds., *The Changing Conversation in America* (Thousand Oaks, CA: Sage Publications, 2002); Geoffrey Nunberg, *Going Nucular: Language, Politics, and Culture in Confrontational Times* (New York: Public Affairs, 2004); Stephen Miller, *Conversation: A History of a Declining Art* (New Haven, CT: Yale University Press, 2006); and Sherry Turkle, *Reclaiming Conversation* (New York: Penguin Books, 2015).

hSee, for example, Rachel LeGoute and Don Everts, *My Digital Voice: An Introduction to the Digital Conversation Pledge*, Lutheran Hour Ministries, 2019, www.lhm.org/pledge.

## EXPLICITLY CALLED TO
## LOVE EVERYONE ALWAYS

As I've already noted, the world that was created and celebrated as "very good" fell, and all that could be shaken and cracked was. In Genesis 3 we see unloving behavior (like hiding and blaming), which is quickly followed in Genesis 4 by murder, an act that at its core exhibits a horrible lack of love.[4] How quick was the fall from love.

It turns out love in a fallen world is tough. When we separate ourselves from God (the source of all love, remember), fallen humanity defaults not to love but to anger and jealousy and defensiveness. After the fall love didn't come naturally, and so God began to explicitly *call* humans to love each other.

At its core the law God gave his people was a call to love. Jesus summarized the entire law as a call to "love your God" and to "love your neighbor" (Matthew 22:37-40). The first four commandments of the Ten Commandments show us how to be in a loving relationship with God, the last six show us how to be in loving relationships with each other. In the law God explicitly called humanity back to what they were created for: to love and to be loved.

And when Jesus came, he reiterated this call and showed how he came to make it possible: "This is my commandment, that you love one another as I have loved you" (John 15:12). This call for Jesus' disciples to love was rooted in Jesus' love for them. As one of Jesus' disciples would cleanly state it, "We love because he first loved us" (1 John 4:19). Jesus' love, expressed most fully in his sacrificial death, made it possible for his disciples to live lives of love. And Jesus was explicit that this call was to *love everyone always*. In a fallen world this has to be expressed explicitly. It can be hard to love mean people or strangers or, worse yet, your enemies. It can be hard to love when life is difficult, as I learned in fifth grade on the playground. And yet Jesus called his followers not just to love people who loved them or when it came easily but to love *everyone always*. Jesus called his disciples to love even their enemies.

This was not folksy naiveté on the part of Jesus (not realizing what goes down on the elementary playgrounds of this rough-and-tumble world), it is divine sophistication (remember, John opens his Gospel by telling us that Jesus was there in the beginning and had an active role in creating humans to love and be loved).

In this fallen world Jesus' invitation to love everyone always is a call to a seemingly upside-down way of life. Jesus knew this. He knew that we are tempted to withhold love from enemies especially. At one point he quoted a popular expression of his day: "You have heard that it was said, 'You shall love your neighbor and hate your enemy'" (Matthew 5:43). And, yes, his followers *had* heard that. Diatribes aren't unique to our day and age, it turns out. It just made sense: it's okay to hate your enemies, isn't it? Jesus was pretty clear on this point as he went on: "But I say to you, Love your enemies and pray for those who persecute you, so that you may be sons of your Father who is in heaven. For he makes his sun rise on the evil and on the good, and sends rain on the just and on the unjust" (Matthew 5:44-45).

Here Jesus invokes God the Father's love of all people—whether they are evil or good, just or unjust. This is not to say that God blesses or excuses or won't one day judge evil (Jesus was clear on this too) but that God's default posture toward humans is to be kind toward them and love them. God the Father is "kind to the ungrateful and the evil" according to the Son (Luke 6:35). And this is meant to be a model for humanity.

The earliest Christian leaders repeated this explicit call to love everyone always—including those it was hardest to love. James called the law's command to love our neighbors as ourselves the "royal law" that we are to "fulfill" (James 2:8). And right after Paul called believers in Rome to love each other— "Love one another with brotherly affection" (Romans 12:10)—he then called them to love *everyone*, even their enemies:

> Beloved, never avenge yourselves, but leave it to the wrath of God, for it is written, "Vengeance is mine, I will repay, says the Lord." To the contrary, "if your enemy is hungry, feed him; if he is thirsty, give him something to drink; for by so doing you will heap burning coals on his head." Do not be overcome by evil, but overcome evil with good. (Romans 12:19-21)

This explicit call to love everyone always was clear to the earliest Christians. And they responded to that call.

## Loving Everyone Always in History

The earliest Christians were known for pursuing the common good. This habit was remarkable because they did this not just for and with each other, but even for and with their enemies, the very people who were at times persecuting them. This is perhaps most notable and striking when it comes to the Christian practice of saving and adopting unwanted pagan babies who had been left outside to die.

Throughout the Roman Empire infanticide was a common practice, "justified by law and advocated by philosophers" of the day. "It was common to expose an unwanted infant out-of-doors where it could, in principle, be taken up by someone who wished to rear it but where it typically fell victim to the elements or to animals and birds."[a]

This practice may sound gruesome to our ears but thought leaders of the time saw no problem with it. Seneca viewed drowning children at birth as both "reasonable and commonplace," and both Plato and Aristotle recommended infanticide as "legitimate state policy."[b]

It is a matter of history that the Christians of the time absolutely prohibited infanticide.[c] But even more remarkable is the fact that Christians, responding to the explicit call to love everyone always, made it their practice to save discarded babies from the garbage heaps outside of town and raise them as their own. The beauty of such acts of love is magnified by the fact that in many cases they were saving the babies of the very neighbors who were persecuting, maligning, and insulting them for being Christians.

In this way and others, the earliest Christians endeavored to stand shoulder to shoulder with their neighbors and love everyone always. As Bishop Cyprian proclaimed at the time, "there is nothing remarkable in cherishing merely our own people with the due attentions of love." Rather, as Cyprian went on, they knew it was possible to "overcome evil with good" by "practicing a merciful kindness like that of God" by loving their enemies as well.[d]

1. What do you think some of the reasons were that early Christians explicitly prohibited infanticide even though it was a common, accepted practice?

2. How might it be emotionally complicated for Christians to save and raise a baby that was discarded by someone who had done them harm?

3. What impression do you think these Christian adoptions had on their pagan neighbors? How might this "heap burning coals on their heads" as Paul put it in Romans?

---

[a]Rodney Stark, *The Rise of Christianity: How the Obscure, Marginal Jesus Movement Became the Dominant Religious Force in the Western World in a Few Centuries* (Princeton, NJ: Princeton University Press, 1996), 118.

[b]Stark, *Rise of Christianity*, 118.

[c]Stark, *Rise of Christianity*, 124.

[d]Stark, *Rise of Christianity*, 212.

This Christian practice of loving enemies is inspiring and underscores just how revolutionary and powerful the explicit call to love everyone always really is. An inaccurate understanding of love would see Jesus' call to love as something nice or well-meaning or sweet. The call to love everyone always is as radical as it is refreshing, as costly as it is beautiful.

And in this fallen world where it's acceptable to "hate your enemies," where our flesh tempts us to punch back at people who have been mean to us, we need to be reminded of the call to love constantly. And God, in his mercy, does just that.

## GRACIOUSLY REMINDED TO
## LOVE EVERYONE ALWAYS

Christians in Asia Minor in the AD 60s lived in a difficult time. There was hostility toward Christians that would, in a few short years, give way to even more violent persecution when Nero would (falsely) blame Christians for starting a fire that devastated Rome. After that, the empire's policy toward Christians would allow for devastating violence against them.

But even in the early 60s, simmering hostility was cause for suffering. Christians endured insults, defamation of character, and verbal abuse regularly—a particularly painful type of persecution for people living in an honor-and-shame culture.[5] This verbal abuse resulted in economic consequences for Christians as well, as their neighbors boycotted their businesses, a practice actively encouraged by their non-Christian business competitors.

This hostility toward Christians wasn't isolated in Asia Minor. Throughout the early church there were seasons of hostility (or outright persecution) that Christians had to navigate. Paul was right when he wrote to young Timothy to be aware that sometimes the gospel would be "in season" and at other times "out of season" (2 Timothy 4:2). Sometimes the winds would blow fair upon Christians and their message; at other times it would blow harsh and hostile.

Why such hostility? Much of first-century Greco-Roman society marginalized Christians simply because they were different.[6] Jewish and Gentile Christians inexplicably fraternized, for example. And rumors about Christians were rampant. Historians from the time characterized Christianity as a mischievous superstition and Christians themselves as a race detested for their evil practices.[7] What evil practices? The practice of baptism sparked ill-informed rumors about drowning babies, and the Lord's Supper (eating flesh and drinking blood, you say?) sparked rampant rumors of cannibalism.

How were Christians supposed to deal with such unwarranted hostility? Many felt the temptation to push back against the hostility, to punch back at their enemies. This, in part, is why Peter wrote his letter. One of the main themes of the letter is that Christians very well may suffer because of their faith. Peter addresses the letter to "elect exiles" and deals head-on with the issue of suffering throughout the letter. According to Peter, Christians in Asia Minor needed to reorient their self-understanding, coming to terms with their status as exiles in their own home towns.[8] At one point, Peter gets very clear about the inevitability of seasons of suffering as Christians, writing, "Beloved, do not be surprised at the fiery trial when it comes upon you to test you, as though something strange were happening to you" (1 Peter 4:12).

And if it is a season of suffering, how should they respond? Peter says, "Finally, all of you, have unity of mind, sympathy, brotherly love, a tender heart, and a humble mind. Do not repay evil for evil or reviling for reviling, but on the contrary, bless, for to this you were called, that you may obtain a blessing" (1 Peter 3:8-9).

What a high and beautiful and costly reminder. Imagine what it would be like to be suffering for your faith and then be reminded that you should bless (yes, bless!) the very people who are attacking you. Given the fact that we all have our own enemies today, let's try to imagine how these words might have landed on the ears of the original recipients of the letter.

## Loving Everyone Always in Asia Minor

*I feel like an outsider in my own land. I am Gordius, and this is my village, Diyarbakir. I can walk from my home to the mighty Tigris River in fifteen minutes. The same river I swam in as a child. The same river my own children swim in today. This is my home. But it feels like the ground has shifted under my feet.*

DIYARBAKIR,
CAPPADOCIA
SUMMER, AD 62

*When we first heard the news about Jesus, God placed inside us the seed of faith. Our lives were changed forever. For me, God's love overcame me.*

*My friends and family didn't understand. How could Gordius, a pagan from birth, go to morning prayers with Jews? My neighbors were curious. The Jewish leaders were concerned. The pagan priests became cold and quiet toward me. There was some confusion and even anger. But not much in those early days.*

All that is changed now. The winds have begun to shift.

Jesus' way is not the normal way—neither pagan nor Jewish. And it doesn't help that Emperor Nero casts a doubtful gaze at Christians. Many of the harsh winds blowing at us have been heated by Nero.

The change in winds has caused a change in my heart. I find anger growing within me. In the market, Sachi, who has never been a friend, mumbled the word cannibal with disgust and spat on the ground as I walked by two weeks ago. I looked up and met his staring eyes. I stopped. My hands clenched. Cannibal? There were many words I wanted to spit right back at Sachi. I held his gaze. And my tongue.

The gathered crowd watched me and Sachi. They know me. They know I, Gordius, have never been shy with my words or my fists. But as I stood there staring at Sachi (imagining all sorts of angry words), a few words from the new letter from Peter came to my mind. This letter has been read at morning prayers ever since it arrived from Galatia some days ago. As I clenched my fists, these are the words from this letter that came into my mind: "Do not repay evil for evil" (1 Peter 3:9).

The words are simple. But their meaning had the power to interrupt my anger. I like payback, you see. But Peter's words are simple and clear. As followers of Jesus we cannot return evil for evil. Instead, we are to bless. Jesus calls me to bless Sachi, to pray for Nero and all of my neighbors.

*I long for days past when we were surrounded by curiosity and kindness. When the way of Jesus was received as good news. But those days are gone. My fists clench when I walk down the streets of Diyarbakir. And Peter's words follow me wherever I go.*

1. How would living in an honor-and-shame culture change how insults or suspicion or distrust feel?
2. What are some of the different ways Gordius could have punched back at Sachi or Nero?
3. Think of a time when you felt distrusted or maligned because you are a Christian. What did it feel like? Were you tempted to punch back in any way?

As we consider what it must have been like to receive and reckon with Peter's letter and its gracious reminder to love everyone always, it's worth remembering that Peter himself knew intimately the temptation to repay evil for evil and reviling for reviling.

Recall it was Peter in the Garden of Gethsemane who pulled out a sword and attacked the high priest's servant when soldiers came to arrest Jesus (John 18:10). And when Peter cut off Malchus's ear, Jesus was unambiguous—he didn't congratulate Peter, he corrected him, "Jesus said to Peter, 'Put your sword into its sheath'" (John 18:11). Peter knew all about the desire to punch back. Perhaps this is why he is so clear and blunt and comprehensive in his directive: don't pay back evil for evil, don't pay back reviling for reviling.

This advice may seem upside down and difficult, but it is the way of Jesus. In his letter Peter points to Jesus himself as the example of this refreshing, unexpected Christian response to hostility:

> For to this you have been called, because Christ also suffered for you, leaving you an example, so that you might follow in his steps. He committed no sin, neither was deceit found in his mouth. When he was reviled, he did not revile in return; when he suffered, he did not threaten, but continued entrusting himself to him who judges justly. (1 Peter 2:21-23)

There's a reason Peter's words haunted Gordius—they are haunting words. The call to bless means it's not enough for Gordius and those like him to just silently clench their teeth and seethe inside. Instead, it's a call to maintain an inner attitude that would allow them to speak well of and sincerely pray for the well-being of their enemies.[9] It's a reminder to love everyone always. To be kind to all, just like God the Father.

This was a reminder that believers living in Asia Minor in the early 60s desperately needed to hear. Peter's letter came just in time. It may be that it is a reminder ideally suited for our time as well.

## LOVING EVERYONE ALWAYS TODAY

Christians in America today may not be suffering as much as Gordius or those Christians after him who suffered under

Nero's more intense persecution, but Christians in the West are definitely in a different season than we've been in for a while.

Cultural observers and researchers (both Christian and non-Christian) have begun to study this massive paradigm shift going on in the West called postmodernity.[10] Among the many findings are those related to the Christian church in the West undergoing a transition from being at the center of society to being at the margins, and Western society undergoing a transition from being Christianized on the whole to being post-Christian on the whole.[11]

To use Paul's terminology, for about three hundred years in the West the gospel was "in season," but since the early 1900s Christianity seems to be a little less so with every passing year. While Christianity is still very much in season (compared with many other places in the world today), the latest research confirms and quantifies what most Christians in the West feel intuitively: this shift to a more post-Christian culture is uncomfortable for Christians.

While the discomfort Christians are feeling is very real and needs to be acknowledged and accounted for, it bears noting that these greater cultural shifts are not necessarily the result of a nefarious evil conspiracy. As Paul wisely observed, there are going to be different seasons for the gospel—that's just the nature of life on fallen earth. In addition, it bears noting that at times we Christians can be part of the cause of our culture's venom or apathy toward the gospel—sometimes we are our own "worst enemies."[12] In fact, some have argued that Christianity's decline in the West is simply a predictable product of choices we Christians have made.[13]

While the state of Christianity in the West is nowhere near as precarious and dangerous as it is in many places in the world today, it is nonetheless true that Christianity in the West has entered into a tougher season. And what is it like for Christians to experience a change in seasons like this? Research shows that a decent percentage of Christians today feel misunderstood (65%), persecuted (60%), marginalized (48%), silenced (46%), and afraid to speak up (47%) because of their Christian faith.[14]

The ground we Christians have taken for granted is shifting beneath our feet, and just like Gordius, we feel this shift personally.[15] Sometimes we don't merely feel displaced, we feel personally injured—whether we've been injured or not.[16] The truth is, there's probably less to be afraid of than we think, as our first year's research into spiritual conversations revealed.[17] And yet many Christians today find the shifts in culture to be enormously frightening and disturbing.[18] We *feel* a sense of displaced heritage, second-class citizenship, and menacing external threats.[19] Even if all these feelings are a bit overwrought, we, understandably, want to do something about it.[20] And sometimes, if we're honest like Gordius, the something we want to do is punch back in some way.

This is why Peter's letter comes at the perfect time for us, just as it did to all those in Asia Minor in the early 60s. Right when some of us are tempted to feel anger and bitterness, Peter's words arrive to arrest our fears and haunt our days: *Love. Everyone. Always.*

Paul wrote that it was possible to "overcome evil with good" (Romans 12:21). What if we made that our default strategy today? Rather than throw our energies into culture wars that often contain "an implicit yet imperious disregard for the goal of a common life," why not throw our energies into loving everyone always by standing shoulder to shoulder with our neighbors and pursuing the common good? [21]

Just as I've imagined Gordius had his clenched fists interrupted by Peter's words, what if we dealt with our own hostile-feeling season by allowing Peter's words (and Jesus' words) to interrupt our fearful postures and call us to stand shoulder to shoulder with our neighbors in a positive, loving pursuit of the common good?

The latest research indicates that this is not a big emphasis in our churches right now. As you can see in figure 3.1, almost no pastors indicated that civic engagement was a top priority for their church. And only 5 percent listed community engagement as a top priority.

If it's true that we can discern someone's priorities based on what they count, then the picture becomes even clearer: joining with our neighbors to bless our communities is not a priority in

# Top Church Priorities

RANKED #1    RANKED #2    RANKED #3

**Worship**
29%
11%
10%

**Teaching / preaching**
27%
17%
13%

**Discipleship**
25%
28%
13%

**Evangelism or outreach**
11%
19%
22%

**Community engagement**
5%
11%
18%

**Relationship building**
2%
7%
8%

**Missions**
1%
6%
15%

**Civic engagement / activism**
0%
1%
1%

*n*=508 U.S. Protestant pastors, July 25–August 13, 2019.

**FIGURE 3.1**

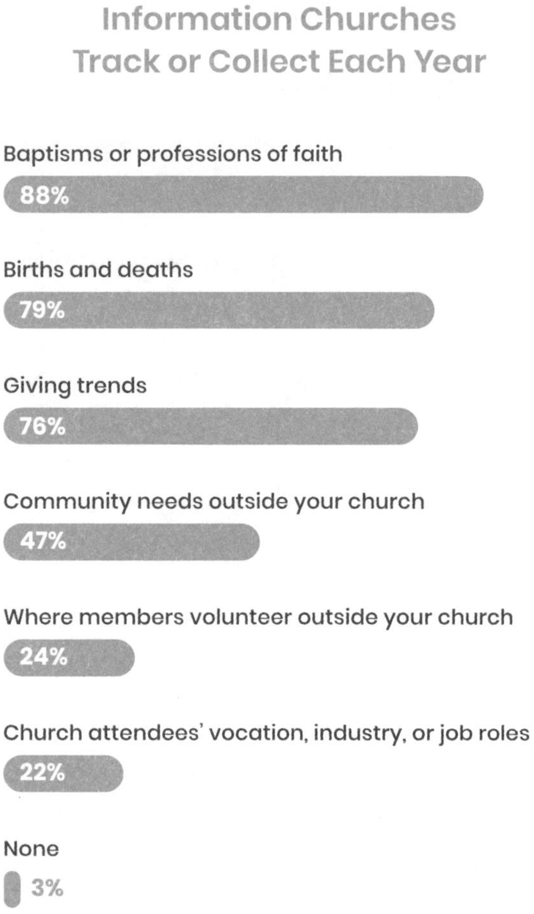

# Information Churches Track or Collect Each Year

**Baptisms or professions of faith**

88%

**Births and deaths**

79%

**Giving trends**

76%

**Community needs outside your church**

47%

**Where members volunteer outside your church**

24%

**Church attendees' vocation, industry, or job roles**

22%

**None**

3%

*n*=508 U.S. Protestant pastors, July 25–August 13, 2019.

**FIGURE 3.2**

our churches. As figure 3.2 illustrates, while the overwhelming majority of all churches are (perhaps wisely) collecting data on baptisms or professions of faith, births and deaths, and giving trends, less than half of all churches are tracking community needs outside the church and a mere 22 percent of churches seem to take an interest in the vocation (and therefore unique giftedness) of those who attend.

> **1.** Have you ever felt misunderstood, persecuted, marginalized, silenced, or afraid to speak up because you are a Christian? How often have you felt this way?
>
> **2.** If you were to list the top five priorities of your church, what would they be? What types of information or data does your church track each year?
>
> **3.** In our current season, what are some of the potential pros and cons of shifting more attention and focus onto working with our neighbors to pursue the common good?

Perhaps we, just like the Christians living in Asia Minor in the first generation of the church, need to be interrupted by Peter's clear letter and Jesus' upside-down call to love everyone always. Could this be the path toward overcoming evil with good? This is something Jessica Crye and her friends have been learning about firsthand.

## Love in Henderson County

In 2012 Jessica and some of her friends from church in Henderson County, Texas, heard about a

HENDERSON COUNTY, TX
2012

sixty-three-year-old local man who was in need financially. He had just learned that he had a detached retina, and without the $20,000 for surgery, he had resigned himself to impending blindness. No longer able to work as he used to, he was having difficulty paying his rent or even buying groceries for him and his wife.

It may not seem surprising that Jessica and her friends at church felt called to use the gifts and resources God had entrusted to them to help their neighbor in need. And they did—reaching out to him to find out what he needed and giving him money that people in their church donated. Nothing too surprising on the surface for a group of Christians who know they are created and called to pursue the common good in exactly this way. Not surprising unless you knew the particular sixty-three-year-old man in need.

Patrick Greene was an outspoken atheist who had been filing complaints and lawsuits for thirty years accusing government officials of unconstitutionally endorsing

Christianity.[a] Earlier that same year he had sued Henderson County arguing that they should remove the nativity scene that always graced the courthouse lawn in December each year. Everyone in Henderson County knew that Patrick was an outspoken atheist activist who saw Christians as "narrow-minded individuals who had treated him unkindly throughout his life."[b]

But this didn't keep Jessica or her friends from loving their neighbor. In fact, their initial gift wasn't the end of the story. Christians in the community got wind of this refreshing example of loving everyone always and chipped in as well, giving thousands of dollars to Patrick and his wife to help with their needs. If the community was shocked at this beautiful act of kindness, Patrick was flabbergasted, saying at one point, "I thought I was in the Twilight Zone."[c]

Being loved by his "enemies" had a tremendous effect on Patrick. He began sharing the story and stated at one point that he wanted to show his appreciation for Jessica and her friends' generosity by buying a star for the top of the manger scene on the courthouse lawn![d] As Patrick put it, "I got all caught up in the excitement. . . . It's easy to do when you get ostracized and treated like garbage. When you're an atheist, you're public enemy No. 1."[e]

Jessica and her friends were simply doing what they are created and called to do: love everyone always—even "public enemy number one." In our day and age this is just as refreshing and surprising and beautiful as ever.

1. Some Christians expressed resentment to Jessica because she had helped such a vocal atheist. Why do you think that is?

2. Who in your local community would you say feels "treated like garbage"? Why is that?

3. What are some different ways you could join with your neighbors in loving that person? What are the barriers that would keep you from doing that?

---

[a]Abe Levy, "Atheist Had Conversion—Albeit a Brief One," *MySA*, May 3, 2012. www.mysanantonio.com.

[b]Rich Flowers, "Atheist 'Flabbergasted' at Christians' Assistance," *Athens Daily Review*, March 20, 2012.

[c]Flowers, "Atheist 'Flabbergasted' at Christians' Assistance."

[d]Flowers, "Atheist 'Flabbergasted' at Christians' Assistance."

[e]Levy, "Atheist Had Conversion—Albeit a Brief One."

In an age of diatribes it is refreshing and surprising and beautiful when we simply do what we were created and called to do: love everyone always.

But as inspiring as this kind of sacrificial, unexpected love is, can this kind of good really overcome evil, as Paul wrote? Can this upside-down way of love accomplish anything? That's what we turn our thoughts to next.

But before we do, can you imagine it? Can you picture what it would look like if Christians everywhere stopped being surprised by their suffering, fought the temptation to punch back, and endeavored to love everyone always? Just imagine.

What if we brought our feelings of being misunderstood or persecuted or marginalized to God and sought his balm and healing and restorative company rather than the sulfuric company of the embittered?

- Make a list of situations or relationships in your life where you sometimes feel defensive because of your Christian faith.

- Spend time reflecting on whether you are carrying any bitterness toward a person, group of people, or institution because of their posture toward the Christian faith. Before God, repent of your bitterness and ask for the grace to extend forgiveness.

- Spend some time in prayer right now, getting honest with God about how it feels to you to be a Christian in an increasingly post-Christian culture.

What if we became transfixed and puzzled and thoughtful about the gracious words—"Father, forgive them, for they know not what they do"—Jesus spoke while hanging from the cross?

- Commit this sentence to memory right now (if you haven't already) and repeat it to yourself when you are tempted toward anger or bitterness.

- Spend time praying for all the non-Christians in your life. Thank God for them and pray for their well-being.

- If any Christians in your life rail against non-Christians, consider a gracious way of injecting some grace and empathy toward non-Christians the next time they are going off.

What if all those projectile posts and emails and forwards and texts stared back from the screen at us: odd and awkward and so patently un-Christlike?

- Spend time reflecting on digital communication generally and your digital habits specifically. Read or listen to the booklet *My Digital Voice* (found at lhm.org/pledge) to help you do this.

- Repent right now of any mean words you have added to the swirling digital diatribe around us.

- Commit yourself to abstain from any digital messages that lack empathy and kindness, taking the "Digital Conversation Pledge" at lhm.org/pledge.

# Give God Glory

## THE JOY OF PROMOTING GOD'S BRAND

*Let your light shine before others, so that
they may see your good works and give
glory to your Father who is in heaven.*

**MATTHEW 5:16**

was living in the rainy town of Gresham, Oregon, when I
understood for the first time how a person's everyday life can
give you a different impression of their God. I was in high school
and my new speech and debate coach was making me rethink
my teenage dismissal of Christianity and God.

Mrs. Robinson taught my freshman speech class and struck
me from the first day as a careful, dignified, professional teacher.
Mrs. R (that's what all the students called her) was one of those
teachers who controlled a classroom not through yelling and
threats but through authority and high expectations. She was

always dressed fashionably, always spoke kindly, and (it seemed to me) always had perfect posture. She may have been petite, but her presence filled the classroom.

So, when Mrs. R invited me to try out for the speech and debate team, I did. And this one invitation changed the trajectory of my life. Not only did it plant the seeds that would grow, over time, into my eventual life's work, but it also brought me into closer proximity with Mrs. R.

She was an extraordinary coach. Teaching, coaching, correcting, encouraging, challenging—she got the best out of everyone on the team. To be in Mrs. R's close orbit was to grow as a speaker and as a person. And there was an unspoken undercurrent to all of Mrs. R's work—her profound Christian faith. I don't ever remember her talking about her faith to the team, but I knew she was a Christian, and I distinctly remember *seeing* her faith: in how she treated us, in how she dealt with setbacks, in how she sacrificed her time, in how she insisted we treat our "opponents."

Mrs. R believed in me, pushed me, and (this was key at the time) was kind to me. You see, during high school it was just my mom and me living in an apartment together miles from the high school, and we had no car. There were many times when we would get back from a speech tournament and Mrs. R would graciously offer to give me a ride home so I wouldn't have to walk in the dark. As I tumbled my way through predictable high school growing pains, Mrs. R never pried, but she always seemed to have the right word of encouragement or guidance or challenge.

For a kid who had dismissed the Christianity of my youth, the testimony of Mrs. R's whole life made me begin to rethink my impression of God and Christianity. As she served shoulder to shoulder with everyone on the team, her whole way of life spoke to me about her God. It made me rethink my disinterest in Christianity.

Mrs. R has remained a friend into my adult life, and I've had several occasions to thank her for the many ways she blessed me in high school—my time on her team taught me many different skills and life lessons. But chief among them was seeing how joyful it can be for a Christian's way of life to influence how other people see God. Mrs. R's gentle, humble way of drawing students' attention to God just felt right.

Of course, as I grew older, I would encounter all sorts of other ways that Christians try to draw attention to their God— some of them weirder and less gentle than others. But when I eventually got around to studying what the Bible has to say about how God made all of us, I discovered that Mrs. R was on to something. We are made to bring glory to God.

## BEAUTIFULLY CREATED TO GIVE GOD GLORY

The first chapter of the Bible comes to a close with God doing a final survey of all that he has created: "God saw everything that he had made, and behold, it was very good. And there was evening and there was morning, the sixth day" (Genesis 1:31).

Here we have our second *Behold!* in the Bible. The first, remember, was an invitation to pause and take notice of all the good gifts God had entrusted into the hands of humans. In this second one we have an invitation to pause and take notice of the final word God had for all he created: it was very good!

The work of God's hands was "very good." In this sense, his work not only spoke for itself, but it also spoke about its Creator as well. Creation unambiguously declares the glory of God. When we *behold* God's creation our estimation of God can't help but grow. As Paul put it, "[God's] invisible attributes, namely, his eternal power and divine nature, have been clearly perceived, ever since the creation of the world, in the things that have been made" (Romans 1:20).

God's eternal power and divine nature can be "clearly perceived" when we look at what he has created. This is a theme that is threaded throughout Psalms, the worship book of God's people. We read in Psalm 19:1, "The heavens declare the glory of God, and the sky above proclaims his handiwork."

Give God glory: To declare your high opinion of God's goodness and spread his fame to others.

The word *glory* has to do with ascribing honor to God; it has at its root a sense of "opinion" or "estimation."[1] In a sense we give God glory when we celebrate or spread his good reputation. And Genesis tells us that this is what all created things—trees and rivers and humans—are created to do. We are created to sing out about our "very good" Creator.

In the beginning, this just happened. Creation implicitly declared the glory of God, every single piece of creation spoke for God in all his wonder, which fulfilled the purpose they were created for in the first place.[2] Trees clapped their hands (Isaiah 55:12) and mountains sang (Psalm 98:8 NIV) and rivers clapped along in praise as well (Psalm 98:8). Every single piece of creation, whether in the heavens or on earth, spoke about God's goodness.

## Paradigm Shift
### FROM COMMERCIALS TO INFLUENCERS

There has been a paradigm shift going on in the realm of marketing. For decades the advertising industry, understandably, has focused on advertisements. Ads are highly produced pieces of content (whether print, audio, or video) expertly designed to get people to respect a brand more and get people to purchase that brand. Marketers work hard to marry style (making an ad attention-grabbing and memorable) with rhetoric (crafting an ad that convinces people of the worthiness of its brand or product). The default marketing strategy has been the creation of ads that affect what people think of a product.

But that's beginning to change. With the advent of social media, marketers have begun to shift their attention away from shiny produced advertisements toward real human influencers. This trend began with highly visible celebrities (think the Kardashians) using their social media presence to personally promote certain brands or products. The secret sauce of this approach to marketing is authenticity.[a] Having a real human being authentically recommend a product is "highly resonate" when compared to slickly produced advertisements.[b] And businesses have noticed. It is estimated that by 2022, brands will be spending up to $15 billion a year on this new kind of advertising.[c] And since authenticity is the key, companies are now tapping into influencers who aren't widely famous. These new niche influencers can have even more perceived authenticity. This kind of embodied marketing is successful not because influencers are seen as educated experts on a product but because people perceive a "genuine connection" between a real person they know (or know of) and a product.[d] This type of marketing doesn't actually work if it is too slick or forced or ingenuine; it works best when influencers genuinely, authentically like a product.

Given what we read in Genesis, perhaps it's time for Christians to undergo a similar paradigm shift in our approach to influencing people's opinions about God. For years there has been an emphasis on Christians using carefully constructed pieces of evangelistic content (whether a great book or a moving CD) to influence people's opinions of our very good God. Some churches and ministries have even coordinated advertising campaigns, paying to get the gospel message on billboards and television sets and into websites and magazines. The common strategy for bringing glory to God has been highly produced pieces of content.

But what if that changed? What if we tapped into this innate desire to give God glory (declaring and spreading his fame) that was imbedded within every created thing? What if we returned to Jesus' radical strategy of calling all his followers to be witnesses, brand influencers within their own family and social networks? What if we responded to our culture's hunger for authenticity by sharing our own "genuine connection" to God? It is worth noting that our first year of research on spiritual conversations confirmed that non-Christians are most open to hearing the gospel message from close friends and family.[3]

1. In what ways have you experienced brand influencers, whether through traditional ads (featuring famous spokespeople) or through brand influencers on social media?

2. What are some of the pros and cons of a produced-content approach to evangelism?

3. What are some of the advantages of individual Christians serving as brand influencers in their everyday social circles? What are the costs of such an approach to evangelism?

[a]Krishna Subramanian, "Five Influencer Marketing Trends For 2019," *Forbes*, April 3, 2019.

bAudrey Schomer, "Influencer Marketing 2019: Why Brands Can't Get Enough of an $8 Billion Ecosystem Driven by Kardashians, Moms, and Tweens," *Business Insider*, July 15, 2019.

cSchomer, "Influencer Marketing 2019."

dSubramanian, "Five Influencer Marketing Trends For 2019."

## EXPLICITLY CALLED TO GIVE GOD GLORY

In the beginning, worshiping God and drawing attention to his wonder was innate and implicit to every part of creation. Giving glory to God was natural. But when creation fell, even this core instinct got shaken and cracked. While rocks and trees and rivers still implicitly declared God's glory, God had to explicitly call humans to do this.

We see this in the explicit call to worship God—to declare his goodness—found throughout the Old and New Testaments. We also see this in the call to spread God's fame to others. God explicitly calls his people to not only worship him but to invite others into that worship. This is why God placed his nation, Israel, "in the center" of all the nations (Ezekiel 5:5)—so that every family on earth could hear about the God of Israel. This is also why Jesus sent out his disciples as witnesses "in Jerusalem, and in all Judea and Samaria, and to the end of the earth" (Acts 1:8)—so that all the nations could hear about the gospel of Jesus through his followers.

God's people are not only called to give God glory by worshiping him but also by inviting other people to worship him as well. We are God's brand ambassadors, if you will, explicitly called to be influencers who offer to the world around us an authentic message about God as Creator, Redeemer, and Savior. We aren't called to market God by spinning slick messages about him but instead to authentically live our faith in ways that people can learn about our God by looking at our way of life. This is exactly how Mrs. R drew my attention back to God.

We are called to do this in both word and deed: sometimes through a spoken message, other times through a lived-out message. It was this important *spoken* message that our first year of research focused on. But it was this *lived-out* message Jesus was referring to in his Sermon on the Mount when he said,

> You are the light of the world. A city set on a hill cannot be hidden. Nor do people light a lamp and put it under a basket, but on a stand, and it gives light to all in the house. In the same way, *let your light shine* before others, so that they may *see your good works* and *give glory to your Father* who is in heaven. (Matthew 5:14-16, emphasis added)

Jesus was unambiguous: when people see his followers' good works, they will naturally give glory to God. In word and deed Christians function as brand influencers who show the people around them an authentic message about God's goodness. This lived-out message is what I received from Mrs. R in high school and is exactly what we see in the early church: their everyday lives gave God glory.

## Giving God Glory Throughout History

We have already looked closely at how the early Christians responded to deadly epidemics and inhumane infanticide. These Christians, often at great cost to themselves, were zealous for the common good and pursued it in the name of Jesus. And what was the result of all this sacrificial love? As we've seen, they literally saved lives and benefitted their local communities in profound ways. But one other result of all this love was that it brought glory to God as a lived-out message.

An early Christian leader Origen (AD 184-253) wrote that the whole world was like a theater filled with spectators watching Christians to see how they would respond to persecution, a common understanding among Christians at the time.[a] In light of this, Origen understood apologetics (the defense of the faith) not to be about rhetoric and ideas but obedience and everyday lives. As he put it, Christ "makes his defense in the lives of his genuine disciples, for their lives cry out the real facts."[b]

Consider that the earliest apologists didn't write arguments about the faith or fashion clever answers to pagan's questions. Instead they "wrote extensively on behavior because of their Christian conviction that the way people live expresses what they really believe."[c]

What did their neighbors think of their behavior? Seeing their actions, their neighbors were "deeply impressed" by their "eloquent behavior," their "exceedingly attractive" patience, and their "wonderful and confessedly striking method of life."[d] Even Christians' enemies had to admire their "benevolence towards strangers."[e]

And all this ultimately brought attention and glory to God. Minucius Felix observed in the early 200s that the Christians' "beauty of life" encouraged "strangers to join the ranks."[f] It was just as Jesus said: when people saw their good works, they would give God glory. The Christians' witness made their neighbor's eyes open wider, made their vision of God grow, and ultimately attracted them to the gospel. As another early Christian writer, Tertullian, wrote in those early years, "It is our care of the helpless, our practice of loving kindness that brands us in the eyes of many of our opponents. 'Only look,' they say, 'look at how they love one another!'"[g]

Ultimately pagans throughout the Roman Empire wanted to join the ranks of Christians because their good works convinced the pagans of the veracity of their message. In this way through both word and deed the earliest Christians spread God's fame, giving him glory.

1. Given what we've seen so far, what do you think was most attractive about the early Christians' lives?

2. How would you summarize the lived-out message non-Christians perceived when they inspected the lives of their Christian neighbors?

3. What conclusions might non-Christian neighbors draw about the Christian faith if they inspected your life?

[a]Alan Kreider, *The Patient Ferment of the Early Church: The Improbable Rise of Christianity in the Roman Empire* (Ada, MI: Baker Academic, 2016), 19.

[b]Kreider, *Patient Ferment of the Early Church*, 94.

[c]Kreider, *Patient Ferment of the Early Church*, 94.

[d]Rodney Stark, *The Rise of Christianity: How the Obscure, Marginal Jesus Movement Became the Dominant Religious Force in the Western World in a Few Centuries* (Princeton, NJ: Princeton University Press, 1996), 165; Kreider, *Patient Ferment of the Early Church*, 2; Kreider, *Patient Ferment of the Early Church*, 23; and James Davison Hunter, *To Change the World: The Irony, Tragedy, and Possibility of Christianity in the Late Modern World* (New York: Oxford University Press, 2010), 284.

[e]Stark, *Rise of Christianity*, 83-84.

[f]Minucius Felix, quoted in Kreider, *Patient Ferment of the Early Church*,123.

[g]Tertullian, *Apology* 39, quoted in Stark, *Rise of Christianity*, 87.

While it is a matter of historical fact that the early Christians gave God glory both in clear word and inspiring deed, the reality is Christians sometimes still need to be graciously reminded that this is what we are called to do. Sometimes we're tempted to grow quiet (and lose the word part), and at other times we're tempted toward selfishness or withdrawal (and lose the deed part). This is why God graciously reminds his people, when they need it, that they are beautifully created and explicitly called to give God glory.

## GRACIOUSLY REMINDED TO GIVE GOD GLORY

We see this clearly among the Christians living in Asia Minor in the AD 60s. Given the tough season they were going through, it makes sense that they would be tempted to isolate themselves from, if not become outright adversarial with, their neighbors.

Peter understood this, but he also understood that their pursuit of the common good would speak louder than any biting words they were tempted to lob back at their neighbors. As Peter put it in his letter, "Beloved, I urge you as sojourners and exiles to abstain from the passions of the flesh, which wage war against your soul. Keep your conduct among the Gentiles honorable, so that when they speak against you as evildoers, *they may see your good deeds and glorify God* on the day of visitation" (1 Peter 2:11-12, emphasis added).

Peter is simply repeating Jesus' words from the Sermon on the Mount: when your neighbors see your good works, they will give glory to God. The behaviors of the Christians are in themselves a sort of message. A message that is not just unexpected and intriguing but can influence how others think about God. This is exactly what Mrs. R's actions did for me.

Peter understood that Christian deeds were a powerful part of their witness. But he also understood that sometimes those deeds needed to be interpreted with words. Consider another encouragement in Peter's letter: "In your hearts honor Christ the Lord as holy, *always being prepared to make a defense to anyone who asks you for a reason for the hope that is in you*; yet do it with gentleness and respect" (1 Peter 3:15, emphasis added).

Peter invited these Christians to gently and respectfully give an answer for the hope that was inside of them. He understood that eventually people would try to puzzle out why these Christians were behaving so differently. They weren't defending themselves or striking back verbally at their accusers—a humble response that would have been startling within the culture in Asia Minor and would have given people pause.[4] And when people asked the Christians why they were so calm and hopeful while suffering, Peter wanted them to explain their actions with gentle and respectful words about the source of their hope, just as Peter did at the beginning of his letter when he wrote that Christians had been "born again to a living hope through the resurrection of Jesus Christ from the dead" (1 Peter 1:3). When the Christians' everyday lives (which were grounded in grace) inevitably attracted the attention of their neighbors, Peter wanted them to interpret their deeds with gentle and respectful words about the gospel of Jesus.

Peter's reminder makes complete sense given that we are created and called to give God glory—spreading his fame through our words and deeds. But given how tempting it is to respond differently during tough seasons, let's try to imagine how this reminder must have landed on the ears of the original recipients of his letter.

## Giving God Glory in Asia Minor

*I think about words as I watch the waters slide by. I am Agatha, and this is my water, the Bosporus.*

HAYDARPAŞA,
BITHYNIA
WINTER, AD 62

I'm thirteen years old. I've spent all my life traveling across this water. My father ferries people back and forth across the Bosporus with his sturdy kayik. My older sister, Nerissa, and I help my father prepare the kayik in the morning. And we clean it at the end of the day. All day long we cross back and forth between Byzantium and all its wonders, and our humble Haydarpaşa.

It is my job to bring water and figs to the passengers. That is what my father tells me. But really I am there to talk with the passengers. To calm those who are nervous. To chat with the excited. To comfort the sick. Not everyone is used to being on the water, so it makes a difference to have a kind word, a little water, a silly joke from a thirteen-year-old girl to distract them. And that is my job while father instructs the oarsmen and Nerissa takes the fares.

I like this job. I love the water, the wind, the activity at the ports. I love the glimpses of exotic Byzantium I get while docked on the far side of the water. I thank God for this job, for father's kayik, for my baby brothers back at home. At the evening prayers I thank God for all he gives me.

But lately I am confused. And that is why I am thinking so much about words.

You see, father and mother and Nerissa and the boys and I are Christians. To belong to Jesus is a comfort and delight. But lately I can tell that not everyone is pleased with this. For the last few months we have had fewer customers, and father *says it is because people in Byzantium have found out that we are Christians.*

*I hate to see people turn away with a shake of the head after speaking with my father at the docks. They shake their heads as if father has done something wrong. And they refuse to get into our kayik. I wanted to cry the first few times. But it is happening more and more.*

*Sometimes after shaking their heads, they still get into our kayik if we are the only ferry available. And those times, as we cross the water, it is hard to bring these head shakers cool water and sweet figs. I don't want to offer a word of comfort or a silly distraction. And this is what has me thinking. You see, at the evening time of prayer they read to us from a letter. It is from one of Jesus' leaders, Peter. And Peter wrote that we should be ready to tell people why Jesus gives us hope. And that we should do that a certain way. These are the words I keep puzzling over. We are to tell people about our hope "with gentleness and respect."*

*I know all about gentleness and respect. I know how to care for our travelers. But for the head shakers this is hard for me. It is hard to respect men and women who show my father no respect. It is hard to be gentle with people who are rude to my father.*

*It is especially hard when they want to talk with me as a distraction during the journey. It's easy to offer water with clenched teeth. But how do you offer conversation with clenched teeth? You can't. And so I puzzle over these words: "with gentleness and respect."*

*A week ago, one of the passengers said to me, as I poured him some water, "So is it true that your family worships the Christ?" He said the words with disgust and maybe a little curiosity, I think. "We do," I said. My heart began to beat faster. He drank his water and held his cup out for more. "Is that why your father won't return our insults? I have said some nasty things to him, but he always smiles at me. He is always kind." I nodded, tears of pride coming to my eyes. "Why is that?" he asked. "I've been watching your father for a few weeks now. He is always kind, little one."*

*He said this as if it were a question. I poured more water into his offered cup but was not sure how to answer his question. There was silence between us as he drank more slowly from his second cupful. And then I answered his question.*

*And now, as I watch the water slide by underneath our kayik I remember this from that leader's letter: when people see our good deeds they will give glory to God. I pray that God will give me the words and the heart to love everyone who comes into our kayik. Just like my father does. I pray that they will see God because they happened to step off the shore into our ferry.*

1. Agatha was struck by Peter's call to answer people with "gentleness and respect." What words would you use to characterize common responses when Christians are asked about their faith?

2. Peter's letter invites Christians like Agatha to be prepared to give an answer for the hope that is within them. Describe a time when you have seen a Christian talk about their faith with "gentleness and respect." Describe a time when you have seen a Christian talk about their faith ungently or disrespectfully.

3. If someone asked you why you are hopeful, how would you answer them?

As we consider what it must have been like to be one of the recipients of Peter's letter, it's important to remember how surprising and attractive the Christian life is.[5] In this fallen world, Christians are called to a different way of life, which can function as an intriguing lived-out message for those around us, just as Mrs. R's everyday actions did for me in high school.

For Christians living in the West today, this is a crucial part of our calling to reckon with and embrace. Given the bad press that Christianity can get at times, it is perhaps the perfect time for us to hear this reminder for ourselves and consider how we can bring God glory through our own words and deeds.

## GIVING GOD GLORY TODAY

To say God has a brand might seem a bit glib. And to suggest that he has a branding problem may be understating how far we've fallen from the beginning when every created thing naturally gave God glory. But while the trees are still clapping their hands for God and the rivers are raising a song of praise, some indicators suggest that God's people are not letting their lights shine as they could be. The latest research suggests our lives are not always "exceedingly attractive" to the people around us.

The majority of US adults say people of faith and religious organizations are responsible for the majority of good works in the country,[6] and 72 percent of practicing Christians say the same, as you can see in figure 4.1. So there is some visibility to our lived-out message.

But that visibility is not what it could be. Notice that only 27 percent of non-Christians give people of faith credit for the majority of good works in the country. How do we account for this perception? It could be that we aren't engaged in as many good deeds as we should be. Or perhaps we aren't standing shoulder to shoulder with our neighbors as we pursue the common good? Have we perhaps so isolated ourselves as Christians that our lived-out message isn't being heard by many people?

Thankfully, joining together with others to pursue the common good seems to tap into the shared work that all humans were created for. Notice in figure 4.2 that a majority of participants in successful communities of action found their groups growing in size over time. There is something beautiful and compelling about people who gather together with their neighbors to pursue the common good of their neighborhood; over time it attracts more and more people to this shared work.

# Religion's Relevance in Good Works

- PRACTICING CHRISTIANS
- NON-PRACTICING CHRISTIANS
- NON-CHRISTIANS

70%  45%  27%

People of faith and religious organizations provide the majority of good works in the country. If these organizations didn't exist, those good works wouldn't get done.

A majority of good works would still happen even if there were no people of faith or religious organizations to do them.

19%  36%  48%

$n$=2,500 U.S. adults, July 25–August 15, 2019. Response option "not sure" is not shown above.

**FIGURE 4.1**

# Size of Successful Groups Over Time

*Base: practicing Christian community participants*

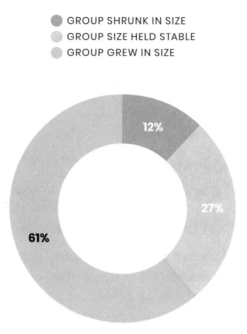

- GROUP SHRUNK IN SIZE
- GROUP SIZE HELD STABLE
- GROUP GREW IN SIZE

12%

27%

61%

*n*=205 U.S. practicing Christian adults who were part of a group, July 25–August 15, 2019. When answering this question, participants were asked to think about the most successful group they'd been a part of.

**FIGURE 4.2**

**1.** According to figure 4.1, Christians and non-Christians have very different perspectives on how engaged people of faith are with good deeds. How do you account for that significant difference?

**2.** How do you think people would have answered this question about "religion's relevance in good works" fifty years ago? One hundred years ago? Two thousand years ago? If you think the answers would have been different, what do you think has changed?

**3.** Why do you think the majority of successful groups that are pursuing the common good tend to grow over time?

Based on the research it would seem that we Christians are due for a gracious reminder to join together with our neighbors in the shared work of pursuing the common good. In a day and age when some of our actions are causing people to be doubtful or dismissive of our faith, the timing couldn't be better to re-capture this call to spread God's fame through both gracious word and inspiring deed.

Perhaps we don't need a new commercial or rhetorical device but rather a simple return to the apologetics of be-havior that fueled the spread of God's fame in the first cen-turies of the church. By returning to this positive, hopeful presence in our neighborhoods, we can perhaps regain the credibility that we once enjoyed.[7] We can spread God's fame through our gentle and respectful words and our loving and sacrificial actions.

The thing is, when we Christians pursue the common good it "speaks loudly about God."[8] This is exactly what Sarah Bernhardt and her husband have discovered.

## Intersect Arts Center

In 2012 Sarah Bernhardt was finishing a graduate degree in art in St. Louis when her husband, Bob, received a pastoral call to serve at Holy Cross Lutheran Church, a historic church in the Gravois Park neighborhood of St. Louis. Gravois Park is home to over five thousand people who represent a vibrant mix of cultures, which creates significant beauty in the neighborhood. But a significant portion of those neighbors is living below the poverty line, which creates obvious struggles.

GRAVOIS PARK, MISSOURI 2012

As it turns out, this historic church owned two mammoth red-brick buildings that were mostly used for storage. So when Sarah graduated she asked if she could clean out one of the many unused rooms to use as an art studio. The church agreed, and Sarah cleaned out an upstairs room and transformed it into a working studio.

One night in summer 2013 she was in her studio when she heard the sound of glass breaking below. She looked out the window and saw two boys down on the street throwing rocks at the windows of the building. They ran away, but later that week, while crossing the parking lot of the large red-brick building Sarah ran into the same boys. Before she could figure out what to say, they began to interrogate Sarah with a mingling of curiosity and distrust.

"Who are you? What are you doing here?" They looked up at Sarah, "Is this a school or something?"

Sarah shook her head, "No. I'm an artist and I have a studio here."

The boys (Sarah figured they were ten to twelve years old) looked confused. Sarah went on, "I make art up in my studio. Do you want to come in and see it?"

Sarah's offer caught the boys off-guard. But they did want to see what she was talking about. So, Sarah showed them around the studio, introducing them to the various tools of the trade. The boys were so intrigued that Sarah asked what is probably a natural question for an artist to ask a neighbor: "Do you want to do an art project together?"

They did. They were thrilled to be invited to do something new and different. So Sarah improvised and came up with an art project that was as redemptive as it was aesthetic. She nodded and smiled, "Great! I tell you what, there's all this broken glass in one of the downstairs rooms.

I think we should clean it up and use those pieces of broken glass for a mosaic project I've been thinking about."

That one art project provided the spark for what eventually became the Intersect Arts Center, a thriving community arts center where Gravois Park neighbors are making beautiful art and having beautiful interactions. When Sarah invited her neighbors to make a mosaic using the pieces from the window they had broken, she had no plans to start a nonprofit or apply for grants or partner with secular and governmental agencies to do a multimillion-dollar renovation! But that's exactly what happened.

Sarah and her husband, Bob, have simply joined together with their neighbors to make mosaics and paintings and sculptures and food and music and fabrics and, over time, a thriving community arts center.

But as they did all that, it turns out they have brought more attention to God. This started with their neighbors—they met kids who lived right across the street from their church who had no idea that it was a church. By standing shoulder to shoulder with them to make art, these neighbors not only found out about their church but more importantly their Christian faith—the reason for the hope inside them.

Eventually people in the artist community throughout St. Louis began to notice what they were doing as well. Artists got involved and eventually became curious about why they were doing what they were doing. One artist in particular (a woman who is estranged from the church and would not consider herself a Christian) was so moved and inspired by Sarah and Bob's words and deeds that, despite the distrust she had for Christianity, she asked a tender question one day: "Can Bob be my pastor?"

Sarah and her neighbors' efforts may have felt messy, unsure, earnest, evolving, and persistent to them, but to others their work seemed like eloquent behavior that, it turns out, has sparked curiosity and surprise from the many agencies they are working with. Leaders from the Regional Arts Commission (a government agency) told Sarah that they had never given to a church before and were surprised that a group of Christians would work hand in hand with non-Christians in promoting the arts. Leaders from the Contemporary Art Museum reached out to find out more about Intersect's work because religious communities had not been represented in their work over the last decades.

Technically, Intersect Arts Center is not a Christian organization. It is a nonprofit that has members and supporters and donors from throughout the community, both Christians and non-Christians joining together to pursue the common good of Gravois Park together. Sarah and Bob's ultimate goal is to have an honest presence as they fulfill their God-given duty of caring for their neighbors and neighborhood. But all these good deeds have formed a lived-out message that, perhaps unintentionally, has caused eyes to grow wider, has drawn attention to God and his church, and ultimately has given God glory.

1. Sarah and Bob's artist friend is estranged from the church and yet wants Bob as her pastor—why do you think that is? Do you know any people who trust you as a Christian but don't trust the church? How do you think they got to that place?

2. What are the potential pluses and minuses that come with Christians partnering with secular and government agencies in their pursuit of the common good?

3. Why do you think it has shocked people that Christians are linking together with non-Christians to pursue the arts?

Should it surprise us that the exceedingly beautiful efforts of people like Sarah and Bob have been noticed not just by their neighbors and partners but by the media and larger society as well? Is it any wonder that the Intersect Arts Center along with Laundry Love, Los Vecinos de Buford Highway, and those generous Christians in Henderson County have all garnered significant media attention? The Christians at the center of each of these stories weren't setting out to become famous, they were just living into what they are created and called to do. But when Christians become zealous for the common good, this is part of what happens—it draws attention to God. It's just like Jesus said: people see our good deeds and give glory to God our Father.

This is exactly what we saw in the first centuries of the church—simple faithfulness surprised the surrounding culture. Sacrifice and love and graciousness, it turns out, are surprising things in this fallen world.

Stories like these make me wonder what's possible if more and more Christians follow suit and become zealous for the common good. What will happen in our lives, in the church, and in our neighborhoods when Christians everywhere unite around the common good? That's exactly what we turn our thoughts to next.

But before we do, just imagine it. Picture what it would look like if Christians everywhere lived as brand influencers, drawing attention to our very good God through gracious words and surprising deeds. Just imagine . . .

What if we had eloquent behavior and God was able to argue the facts of the faith through our lives?

- Make a list of words you would use to describe your behavior (eloquent, attractive, normal, kind, etc.).

- Spend time reflecting on what message your everyday life sends to your neighbors and those in your social circles. What conclusions could people come to about God based on your everyday life?

- In what ways do you wish your behavior was different? Spend time asking God to move in your life. Invite the Holy Spirit to shape you and guide you and convict you and encourage you.

What if the sight of a church steeple triggered not bitter memories of an argument or a crass evangelistic encounter or divisive political rhetoric, but triggered pleasant memories of gracious words and good deeds?

- Spend time right now praying for healing for those folks in your neighborhood who are carrying around church hurt of some kind. Invite the Spirit to bring them peace and healing, to bring them into contact with some "exceedingly attractive" Christian lives.

- For the next week say a short prayer for every church you pass during your day. Pray that God would give the members of those churches favor with the non-Christians in their lives.

- If you know someone who has been hurt by the church or Christians (and have enough trust with them), go and apologize to them on behalf of the church, asking them for forgiveness.

What if Christians were asked regularly and sincerely about the reason for the hope within them?

- Jot down some gentle and respectful words on a piece of paper, wrestling with what you could say when you are asked about the hope within you.

- Learn more about how to be gracious and helpful in your conversations with non-Christians by spending some time learning about the Spiritual Conversation Curve (lhm.org/curve)—a biblical, research-based model for how to graciously adapt to the spiritual posture of the person you are talking to.

- Chart a growth plan for how you can become a more "eager conversationalist" by taking the free online course "Eager to Share" at www.lhm.org/learn.

# Join the Revolution

## THE HOPE OF UNITING AROUND THE COMMON GOOD

*You yourselves like living stones are being built up as a spiritual house.*

**1 PETER 2:5**

I was living within the hilly streets of Tacoma, Washington, the first time I was invited to join a revolution. I was finishing my first year at college when my friend Troy asked if I would join him and his friends in spreading Jesus' kingdom across the University of Puget Sound campus in the fall.

I had been asked to do lots of things by Christian leaders in the past: volunteer, donate, pray to open a meeting, even lead a devotion or two. But I had never been asked to embark on a grand mission like this. Troy was unambiguous: it was a mission so big in scope it would require joining together with others in this shared work. He invited me to partner together with Melinda (a senior at my school) to lead a Bible study in Anderson-Langdon Hall the next fall. And he invited the two of us to meet once a week with a network of other leaders from around campus. Troy was inviting me (I would come to discover over time) to join a global network of Christian students united around the mission of spreading Jesus' kingdom across college campuses all over the globe.

I knew that God's kingdom would one day fully be consummated when Jesus came back in glory, but to be a small part of expanding that kingdom in the here and now? That felt epic to me. No one had ever asked me to do something this large and important and compelling before. I felt simultaneously honored and challenged, excited and scared. I said yes. And it turned out to be incredible.

Partnering with Melinda (especially for an introvert like me) was a revelation. Melinda and I were so different from each other: I was fearful, angsty, and a little too clever for my own good; Melinda was bright, fearless, and full of energy and joy. That next school year I learned so much about my limitations and also a little about my gifts. Melinda was a great partner and coach, and our Bible study really did see Jesus' kingdom advance in our dorm.

Our weekly meetings with other leaders involved sharing war stories from the previous week, celebrating kingdom victories, studying the next week's Bible passage together. I found myself encouraged and sharpened and *braver* after connecting with this network of leaders each week.

And I'll never forget the first time I attended a gathering that included student leaders from around the world who were doing the same thing on their college campuses. We stood together in worship, we sat together to break bread, we studied the Bible together; there was an unforgettable, unmistakable comradery and unity and bold hope that this global network of leaders felt together. It just felt right.

Over the years I've felt the temptation to go it alone and curl in on my fearful, angsty, too clever self. I've felt the temptation to aim lower, pursue more manageable goals. But eventually I am brought back to how right it feels to be called to join a mission so big it requires uniting together with a network of others. And as I read what the Bible says about humanity's creation mandate, I have a sense that there's something right about Troy's invitation back in the day. It turns out we are made to join with others in a mission too large to accomplish by ourselves.

## BEAUTIFULLY CREATED TO JOIN THE REVOLUTION

Genesis not only tells us humanity was created to "work" and "keep" the place and people around us, but it also tells us this shared work had a huge scope—which suggests this is a work no one person can do alone: "God said to them, 'Be fruitful and multiply and fill the earth and subdue it, and have dominion over the fish of the sea and over the birds of the heavens and over every living thing that moves on the earth'" (Genesis 1:28).

Consider the scope of the mandate: fill the *entire* earth, have dominion over *every* living thing. The geographic scope alone is stunning, let alone the expansive purview humans are tasked with. Humanity's original task was to begin in the garden, but ultimately it would work its way outward, eventually spreading the blessings of Eden to all the earth.[1]

The global scale of this mandate is enough to strongly suggest humans obviously will be uniting together to pull this off, whether they recognize where the mandate and their gifts come from or not. It would take many people with many different vocations to fulfill this great mission—ultimately requiring ranchers and farmers, weavers and gardeners, teachers and economists, and leaders and poets and construction workers and nurses. The scope of the mission is so large it calls forth a great, collaborative effort.

If the scope of the global mandate *implies* humanity will need to unite in this task, then God's observation that it is not good for Adam to be alone because he needs a "helper" is *explicit*: humans need to unite in the grand mission they are charged with. We are all created to join together in the beautiful task of pursuing the common good. And no matter where you live, you are surrounded by people who are created for the same, whether they know it or not.

## Paradigm Shift

### FROM CLASSROOMS TO NETWORKS

A paradigm shift is taking place in the realm of higher education. For decades there has been an emphasis on the professor imparting knowledge and the students receiving that knowledge. Whether through lectures, group discussions, or question-and-answer sessions, a single person is providing the content, instruction, and intellectual shepherding of the students. The default learning experience has been a teacher and students in a classroom.

But that's beginning to change. Increasingly, universities are experimenting with and expanding the use of a very different kind of learning experience, namely, a social learning network.[a] Through online discussions and forums, accountable groups of students are networked with other groups to ask their questions, puzzle through problems, clarify content, and learn from each other and other groups, not just the professor. Student voting and computer algorithms make sure that the most helpful interactions on the forums rise to the top; as a result the crowd "gains its wisdom not from the knowledge of one, but from the collective knowledge of many."[b]

Given what we read in Genesis, perhaps it's time for us to undergo a similar paradigm shift in our approach to blessing our neighborhoods. Rather than limit ourselves to the (albeit considerable) insights and ideas of a small group of neighbors in our neighborhood, what if we networked with other small groups of neighbors from around the country to share our collective (considerably more expansive) insights and ideas?

What if the scale and grandeur of this call to pursue the common good in our neighborhoods pressed us beyond our current limits and forced us to join with a network of other like-minded people?

1. What do you think are the inherent virtues of the classic classroom experience with one teacher?

2. What do you think are the inherent limitations of the classic classroom experience?

3. If a network of people pursuing the common good were to succeed, what would it ideally be like? How would it function?

[a]Christopher G. Brinton and Mung Chiang, *The Power of Networks: Six Principles That Connect Our Lives* (Princeton, NJ: Princeton University Press, 2017), 152.

[b]Brinton and Chiang, *The Power of Networks*, 151.

## EXPLICITLY CALLED TO JOIN THE REVOLUTION

Remember, when Adam and Eve fell into sin and left the garden, they did not leave their global mandate behind. In fact, God was explicit that they were still called to a global purpose. Now, the path to global human flourishing had changed, of course, because of the fall, but the Bible reveals the good news that we'll still get there—when Jesus comes again to reign in glory, we will experience complete and joyful shalom.[2]

But while the path to global human flourishing changed, the original call to pursue shalom did not: God explicitly called his people to be fruitful and multiply in order to bless the entire world. This global mission began with Abraham. God called Abraham and his descendants after him to bless "all the families of the earth" (Genesis 12:3)—the same global scope given in the garden. And this did begin to happen: "The people of Israel were fruitful and increased greatly; they multiplied and grew exceedingly strong, so that the land was filled with them" (Exodus 1:7).

This great mission (and the collaboration it would require) only became clearer and more explicit when Jesus came. Jesus was clear that he had come to announce and inaugurate the kingdom of God (Mark 1:14-15). To the status quo this kingdom was a revolution, a redemption of all that had been cracked and shaken and divided at the fall.

In one sense, Jesus' kingdom was like *a* revolution: it represented an overturning of the fallen ways of the world. But it was also like *the* revolution: a network of like-minded people who labor and sacrifice their lives for that beautiful overturning. Jesus was explicit about this as well. Not only did he call a group of people and form them into a community, but he was also explicit that they were to go forth and announce his kingdom *together*. Recall that Jesus always sent his disciples out in groups—at least in pairs—for the shared work he gave them.

And the leaders of the early church understood all this. Paul, for example, was very clear about the scale of the mission. Quoting Isaiah 49:6 in a sermon in Pisidian Antioch, Paul said,

So the Lord has commanded us, saying,

"I have made you a light for the Gentiles,
that you may bring salvation to the ends of the earth."
(Acts 13:47)

Paul clearly understood that a grand mission like that would require a coordinated network of God's people moving out in a united fashion. The image Paul used to capture and celebrate this was the image of a body: "Just as the body is one and has many members, and all the members of the body, though many, are one body, so it is with Christ" (1 Corinthians 12:12).

Paul expanded on this metaphor at length, making it clear that God's people are not lone wolves or independent operators but rather parts of a coordinated community. And they are all moving and working and laboring in coordination with each other, obedient to the head of the body, Jesus.

God did not call disparate individuals to the global task of blessing every family on the earth—he called a *people*. God formed a *nation* for this purpose and then, through Jesus, formed a *church* for this purpose. God's people were to be like an extended family, a powerful network laboring together for God's purposes. It was as members of *the revolution* that they could be used to further God's revolutionary kingdom.

# Joining the Revolution in History

The earliest Christians understood that the kingdom of God represented a message and a culture that was revolutionary in their world. In a world where pagans viewed mercy and pity as weaknesses, Jesus' call to live mercifully was "new and revolutionary."[a] The Christians' way of loving everyone by serving them was also undeniably "revolutionary stuff" in the ancient world.[b] It was as if the Christians brought into their neighborhoods a new culture that transformed everyday life in obvious ways.[c]

But it also bears noting that Christians weren't just purveyors of revolutionary ideas, they were committed members of *the revolution*. They were united even as they lived out their lives in different locations in the ancient Near East. Traveling teachers like Paul brought inspiring stories and personal words of greeting and encouragement from one church to another: "So that you also may know how I am and what I am doing, Tychicus the beloved brother and faithful minister in the Lord will tell you everything. I have sent him to you for this very purpose, that you may know how we are, and that he may encourage your hearts" (Ephesians 6:21-22).

In Colossians 4 we get a vivid insight into the robust relationships and networks functioning in the early church. In that chapter alone Paul sends the believers in Colossae news or greetings from two other churches (Laodicea and

Hierapolis) and mentions ten partners in ministry (Tychicus, Onesimus, Aristarchus, Mark, Justus, Archippus, Epaphras, Luke, Demas, and Nympha). The church was functioning as a highly fruitful network of people.

Encouraging and convicting epistles (like Peter's first epistle, which we've been considering more closely) were shared between neighboring cities, at times shared from group to group throughout entire regions. Paul added a note at the end of his letter to the church in Colossae: "When this letter has been read among you, have it also read in the church of the Laodiceans; and see that you also read the letter from Laodicea" (Colossians 4:16).

Leaders from various churches would gather to puzzle through problems (Acts 15), share stories of God's work (Acts 11), and even share resources (Acts 11). As the church grew, treatises about the call to love everyone always and exhibit "strange patience" were also written and spread wherever there were Christians. As a single body, the early church was a unified network engaged in fruitful partnerships.

1. What elements of the kingdom of God are inherently revolutionary in your local context today?

2. In what ways have you experienced partnership, encouragement, or inspiration from people in your local church as you are engaged in the work of the kingdom of God? How have you experienced this from Christians outside your local congregation?

3. Is there a Christian outside your local congregation (perhaps someone living far away) that you could encourage in their kingdom work?

---

[a]Rodney Stark, *The Rise of Christianity: How the Obscure, Marginal Jesus Movement Became the Dominant Religious Force in the Western World in a Few Centuries* (Princeton, NJ: Princeton University Press, 1996), 212.
[b]Stark, *Rise of Christianity*, 86.
[c]Stark, *Rise of Christianity*, 162.

The vibrant, active network that existed in the first centuries of the church makes sense given that they were beautifully created and explicitly called to unite with others in a grand mission. But in this fallen world where our sweet tooth for division remains and our horizons tend to shrink, sometimes we need to be reminded to unite with others in the revolution. And God in his mercy does just that.

## GRACIOUSLY REMINDED TO JOIN THE REVOLUTION

For one final time let's return to the network of Christians living in Asia Minor in the mid-AD 60s. While it would be tempting in the face of persecution to hole up and simply try to survive, Peter was careful to remind these believers of where they were heading. In his second letter Peter would remind these believers that they were "waiting for new heavens and a new earth" (2 Peter 3:13) that would be ushered in when Jesus came back in glory. In this first letter he reminds them of this "living hope" and celebrates how they can rejoice in this knowledge of a coming inheritance (1 Peter 1:3-6). In light of where they were heading, Peter wanted these Christians to remember the grand mission they were a part of: "You are a chosen race, a royal priesthood, a holy nation, a people for his own possession, that you may proclaim the excellencies of him who called you out of darkness into his marvelous light" (1 Peter 2:9).

Proclaiming the excellencies of Jesus is indeed a high task they were called to, and Peter wanted them to remember this. But he also wanted them to appreciate that such a high task rightly calls for collaboration with other Christians. After all, they were a part of a greater whole: a race, a priesthood, a nation, a people. Each Christian is a part of a greater network. Peter had a memorable way of picturing this: rather than a picture from the world of anatomy (like Paul's body metaphor), Peter used a picture from the world of construction: "As you come to him, a living stone rejected by men but in the sight of God chosen and precious, you yourselves like *living stones* are being built up as a *spiritual house*, to be a holy priesthood, to offer spiritual sacrifices acceptable to God through Jesus Christ" (1 Peter 2:4-5, emphasis added).

It's a striking picture: each Christian is like a living stone. But not a stone sitting by itself, rather, all these stones are being brought together by God to form a spiritual house. This is a memorable picture of individuals collaborating for a greater purpose: a grand house made up of individual stones.

In practice this could be stunning to see in action. Remember that Asia Minor was not a small homogenous area. All these different "living stones" Peter is writing to were unique and different. The network of churches throughout Asia Minor was made up of both Jews and Gentiles, and Asia Minor itself was composed of a "fantastic conglomeration of territories," including coastal areas, mountain ranges, plateaus, lakes, and rivers.[3] And yet across all that fascinating diversity, Peter was calling them to put their hands together to the single, grand mission God had given them. Peter says, "Finally, all of you, *have unity of mind*, sympathy, brotherly love, a tender heart, and a humble mind" (1 Peter 3:8, emphasis added).

The phrase "have unity of mind" is an important one. In fact, in the Greek it's just a single word: *homophrones*. It literally means "same-minded" and carries the connotation "of one mind, like-minded, united with others in the way one thinks."[4] Peter is inviting these Christians spread throughout Asia Minor to be "linked in common purpose."[5] And his letter is intended to help them to do just that. Peter has addressed the letter to the five regions in Asia Minor, as we see at the beginning of the letter: "Peter, an apostle of Jesus Christ, To those who are elect exiles of the Dispersion in *Pontus, Galatia, Cappadocia, Asia,* and *Bithynia*" (1 Peter: 1:1, emphasis added).

Peter is writing a circuit letter that he is sending with his ministry partner Silvanus (1 Peter 5:12). Through Silvanus the letter is first delivered in Pontus and makes its way to Christians in each region of Asia Minor, successively calling them to be united in common purpose.

What a helpful, inspiring reminder to people who are undergoing persecution. While tempted to hole up and just survive, Peter is lifting their heads to remind them of the grand task before them and the growing network of partners they have in that task. They are a chosen race, a royal priesthood, a people of God, spiritual stones that are being built into something great. They are linked together in a common purpose that is worth their greatest efforts. What a wonderful, timely, and hopeful reminder from Peter.

Given the fact that we too are in a tough season and still have a sweet tooth for division, let's try to imagine, one final time, how these words might have landed on the ears of the original recipients of the letter.

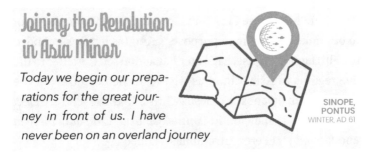

## Joining the Revolution in Asia Minor

*Today we begin our preparations for the great journey in front of us. I have never been on an overland journey*

SINOPE,
PONTUS
WINTER, AD 61

*of any kind, let alone a months-long overland journey. I have plied the waters of the Euxine Sea my whole life, of course— my brothers and I are fishermen by trade. The sea I know. The great expanse of Asia Minor? That is a mystery to me.*

*I am Dilphius and this is my village, Sinope. My brothers and I and all our neighbors in Sinope live here on a thin strip of land surrounded on three sides by the sea. We are on the farthest tip of the land, barely touching Asia Minor at all.*

*And yet my brothers and I will be leaving our familiar village for many months. Silvanus brought apostle Peter's letter to the evening prayer meeting last week. My brothers and I and all the Christians in Sinope have been encouraged in our faith because of that letter. God has used Peter's words to remind us of the excellencies of Jesus. The letter has reminded us of the call on our lives to proclaim those excellencies to our neighbors and those we work with in the fishing trade. But a few of Peter's words stay with me as I mend the nets each night. Peter wrote, "have unity of mind" (1 Peter 3:8). The words are simple in meaning, inviting us to be linked together in a common purpose. But these words took on new meaning when the elders talked with Silvanus about his plans.*

*You see, Peter has given Silvanus the task of bringing this letter throughout the land of Asia Minor. Silvanus is to bring encouragement and greetings and love along with this letter from our Pontus region down to Galatia and the great city of Ancyra, over to the churches in Cappadocia,* all the way to the busy ports of Asia with their famed Roman Roads, and then back up to Bithynia, which lies just across the Bosporus from the great city of Byzantium.

When the elders talked with Silvanus about this grand journey, he asked for companions to help ease the rigors of the road. And the elders have appointed me and my brothers to this task! I'm a simple fisherman, more comfortable on the sea than a mountain pass. I've never been to a city larger than my village.

I have not slept much since the elders met with us. It is an honor, of course. I'm thrilled that they would trust us with such a mission. I'm humbled that I will get to learn from Silvanus and meet brothers and sisters in Christ throughout the land.

But those few words stay with me: "have unity of mind." I know what it is to be linked to others in a common purpose: this is what it is like on the sea while fishing. My brothers and I are shoulder-to-shoulder in the boat, each with a role, each of us relying on the others to fulfill their roles. On the boat we are linked in this great purpose of catching the fish that will feed our families and many in the village.

It is the same at the evening prayer meeting: we Christians in Sinope are linked together in purpose as well. But this journey is different. Bringing this letter throughout the churches of Asia Minor will be like threading together every Christian and every church to the grand mission God has us all on. Like mending a fishing net, we will be joining *all together in a strong net of believers, unified in purpose.*

*Even as we make our preparations, I am filled with excitement and fear. I've never been off this coast. I've never traveled inland. I've heard incredible stories about Ancyra and Byzantium and the busy, sophisticated ports of Asia. But to think that I will be walking on the streets of those cities is almost too much for me. And yet.*

*And yet I feel something stirring deep inside me. Perhaps this hunger for a grand journey has been lying dormant inside me, roused since the elders talked with us. Maybe I've been created to make preparations and embark on a grand journey like this after all.*

*As I mend the nets at night, I wonder: What effect will this letter have in each place we travel to? How will those in Cappadocia be convicted? How will those in Ancyra be comforted? How will the brothers and sisters in Asia change because we are stringing our net of the faithful even that far?*

1. What are some of the different ways it would have been possible for Christians living in different cities in Dilphius's day to be linked together in a common purpose?

2. In what ways is this possible for Christians today?

3. Have you ever felt deep inside you a dormant hunger for a grand journey or mission? What evidence, if any, have you seen that humans are created to take part in a grand mission?

People like the Dilphius I've imagined didn't have the communication technology we have today, and yet they were able to be a part of a robust network of Christians in the ancient Near East who were joined together with unity of mind. Of course, they faced distractions and temptations and fears that could have led to isolation or division, but Peter graciously reminded them of what they had always been meant for: to unite with others in a grand mission.

Given our own temptations toward distraction and isolation and division (and given the powerful network-creating technologies at our fingertips today), what a hopeful moment for groups of neighbors today to rediscover, reclaim, and rekindle this dormant, ancient hunger we all have to be enlisted in a mission larger than we are, a mission that can link our smaller neighborhood groups with similar groups across the country in the same common purpose.

## JOINING THE REVOLUTION TODAY

As we've seen, the Bible reveals that all humans are created for a mission whose scope and grandeur require collaboration and partnership and networking. The latest research confirms this. Researchers described a group of neighbors partnering together in pursuit of the common good and then asked people if they would ever consider joining such a group. Among practicing Christians who have never been in such a group, more than seven in ten said they would either definitely (42%) or probably

# Practicing Christians' Openness to the Church's Help with Finding Groups

**"Would you like for your church to help you find or join a group that addresses one of these causes?"**

*Base: practicing Christians at least somewhat interested in joining a group*

- DEFINITELY
- PROBABLY
- MAYBE
- PROBABLY NOT
- DEFINITELY NOT

### Not community participants

| 35% | 25% | 31% | 6% | 3% |

### Community participants

| 37% | 22% | 28% | 11% | 2% |

*n*=1,005 U.S. practicing Christian adults, July 25–August 15, 2019.

FIGURE 5.1

(30%) join such a group. Another 21 percent said they might join such a group.[6] Among all others (non-practicing Christians and non-Christians) who have never been in such a group the numbers aren't quite as high, but are still considerable: more than four in ten said they would either definitely (20%) or probably (26%) join such a group. And another 41 percent said they might join such a group.[7]

When asked why they hadn't joined such a group yet, the most common answer given was that they hadn't found one.[8] This suggests that people may need practical help to find or form a group of neighbors who are pursuing the common good together. Practicing Christians, for example, are very open to their church helping them find a group of neighbors to pursue the common good. As you can see in figure 5.1, 91 percent of practicing Christians who are not currently in such a group are either definitely (35%), probably (25%), or maybe (31%) open to their church helping them find such a group. The numbers are almost the same among folks who are already in a group—most practicing Christians are open to help from their church in finding or forming a group of neighbors to partner with in their neighborhood.

> **1.** If you have not joined a group of people pursuing the common good of your local community, what would you say is the primary reason? Any secondary reasons?

**2.** What do you imagine are some of the difficulties in finding such a group?

**3.** Why do you think finding a group is the most common barrier?

Finding or forming a group of neighbors doesn't just happen, of course. It requires some kind of purposeful organizing as we see in the early church. To borrow Peter's metaphor (which he was using to talk specifically about the church), each individual living stone must be somehow brought into contact and coordination with all the other stones to build something solid and good. The gifts humanity needs in their shared work are not given to one person or one church, they are given to all people and to the church universal.[9]

So, we need some sort of organizing because this kind of effort will naturally require "collaboration, networking, mutual dependence, and institution-building."[10] It may be fashionable to denigrate structures and institutions, but history shows institutions are essential for the grand goal of human thriving.[11] Groups don't just form and don't just network with other groups magically. It takes purposeful effort and coordination.

On the one hand, this will mean individuals taking the initiative to get the ball rolling. There has to be a first neighbor who stands up and says: Why don't we stand shoulder to shoulder for the good of the place and people around us? The research confirms that this is a message our neighbors, both

# Pastors' View of Lay Leadership

AGREE STRONGLY
AGREE SOMEWHAT
DISAGREE SOMEWHAT
DISAGREE STRONGLY

## "I Prefer Lay Initiatives to New Church Programs"

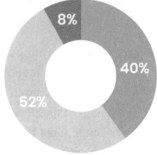

8%
40%
52%

## "For Our Church to Be Healthier, Lay People Must Take More Responsibility"

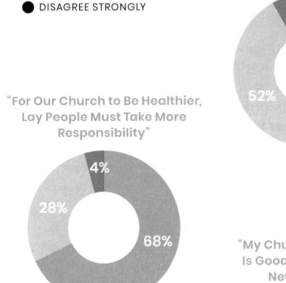

4%
28%
68%

## "My Church Leadership Is Good at Developing New Leaders"

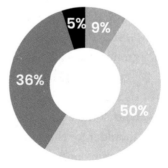

5% 9%
36%
50%

*n*=508 U.S. Protestant pastors, July 25–August 13, 2019.

FIGURE 5.2

# Group Organization in Successful Groups

*Base: practicing Christian community participants*

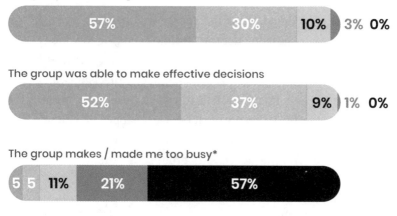

- ● STRONGLY AGREE
- ● SOMEWHAT AGREE
- ● NEITHER AGREE NOR DISAGREE
- ● SOMEWHAT DISAGREE
- ● STRONGLY DISAGREE

**The group was well organized**

| 57% | 30% | 10% | 3% | 0% |

**The group was able to make effective decisions**

| 52% | 37% | 9% | 1% | 0% |

**The group makes / made me too busy***

| 5 | 5 | 11% | 21% | 57% |

*n*=205 U.S. practicing Christian adults who were part of a group, July 25–August 15, 2019. When answering this question, participants were asked to think about the most successful group they'd been a part of. *For this response, the scale was: completely true, mostly true, somewhat true, a little true, not true at all.*

**FIGURE 5.3**

Christian and non-Christian, want to hear, but there has to be someone to bring that message to a neighborhood. Someone has to take the initiative.

There is something beautiful and powerful about everyday people taking the initiative. As you can see in figure 5.2, a wide majority of pastors prefer lay initiatives over new church programs and are convinced that individuals in the church must take that initiative.

On the other hand, these individuals and fledgling groups will need helpful best practices and training and guidance along the way. As you can see in figure 5.3 successful neighborhood groups tend to be well organized, make effective decisions, and don't make their members feel too busy. Helping a group become successful in these ways doesn't just happen, it requires purposeful coordination and training and encouragement. Forming and finding successful groups in pursuit of the common good requires both initiative and coordination.

**1.** Why do you think 92 percent of pastors prefer lay initiatives to new church programs?

**2.** Do you agree or disagree with the statement "For our church to be healthier, lay people must take more responsibility"? What are the possible barriers that keep people from taking the initiative?

**3.** In your experience, what factors determine whether a group will be well run or not?

There's nothing new about the need to pair personal initiative with helpful coordination. Peter's circuit letter undoubtedly had a profound personal influence on each of its hearers, but the coordination and logistics involved to get it around to each region of Asia Minor were what it took for God to use the letter to join people together throughout the region. This more institutional part of pursuing the common good is not optional, it is of "essential importance."[12]

Revolutions always require some sort of structure. While gifted individuals and powerful ideas do shape and change culture, these changes are embedded in culture and passed down to future generations through institutions.[13] It's worth noting that historians believe "the key actor in history is not individual genius but rather the network and the new institutions that are created out of those networks."[14] This should not be too surprising given what the Bible shows us: we were created to put our hands to a mission so grand that it requires networking with others.

In other words, it is a *good* thing when an individual becomes zealous for the common good. And it is a *beautiful* thing when a small group of these people joins together in the same neighborhood. But it is a *profound* and *history-altering* thing when a network brings a bunch of those groups together. Just like Dilphius's scary and exciting overland journey to seed a network across Asia Minor, this network-building "will take creative thinking, imagination, and hard work," but the more active that network is, the more influence it will have over time.[15] This is exactly what Tony Cook and his friends are finding out.

## The Hopeful Neighborhood Project

ST. LOUIS,
MISSOURI
2020

Having grown up in Downs, a small rural community in Illinois, Tony Cook learned the beauty of neighbors helping neighbors. He experienced firsthand how each member of the community, regardless of background, had unique gifts to share. If you needed your car fixed, you took it to Chuck's dad; if your wiring went bad, you called Russ. Tony saw the art of neighboring being practiced everywhere in his community—even in his own home the point was driven home as he watched his dad, better known as Fuzzy, put on his boots and Carhartt jacket time and again to come to the aid of a neighbor.

A number of years after leaving his small town, Tony went on to work in the local church and to teach in a seminary only to discover that the Christian community wasn't always like the farming community of Downs. Instead, he frequently discovered that Christians can be prone to huddling. He realized how isolated from (and even dismissive of) their neighbors Christians can be. In 2017, Tony began to dream about the church in America. What would it be like if Christians participated in their neighborhoods like his neighbors back in Downs? What would it be like if Christians pursued the common good with their neighbors right where God had placed them?

And so when Tony was designing a three-year research project that would direct the bright spotlight of the Barna Group and Lutheran Hour Ministries on important areas of the Christian experience today, he decided to explore these neighborhood-related questions. Tony assembled a team and together they dove into the research and began exploring the implications of that research. This book is one part of that effort.

One key finding was what we have been exploring in this chapter: Christians and non-Christians alike are hungry to make a difference in their neighborhoods. But they need help in figuring out how to join with others to do that. Out of this important finding the Hopeful Neighborhood Project was born.

The Hopeful Neighborhood Project is a brand-new collaborative network launched by Tony and his team that is committed to improving neighborhood well-being around the world. Their resources and online network equip and encourage neighbors to work together, using their gifts and the gifts of their community, to pursue the common good of their neighborhood. The Hopeful Neighborhood Project is founded on not only the conviction that we are all created to pursue the common good but also that we are all created to join with other like-minded people in this shared work. Toward that end Tony and his friends have created practical tools and a global network.

The practical tools include *The Hopeful Neighborhood Field Guide*,[a] a personal gift inventory, neighborhood assessment tools, teaching videos, and more. These tools are designed to help anyone pursue the common good in their neighborhood by gathering a few neighbors and taking three steps together: discovering the gifts, imagining the possibilities, and pursuing the common good.

Their global network is facilitated by a website (hope fulneighborhood.org) that links like-minded people all across the world in a social-learning network. This network allows neighborhood groups a place to find encouragement, best practices, creative ideas, feedback, and even coaching related to pursuing the common good in their own neighborhood. It's also a place for neighborhood groups to share their ideas, insights, and stories with others.

While creating this new collaborative network has indeed required "creative thinking, imagination, and hard work," Tony and his friends know that this is how the world changes. As Tony put it,

In an increasingly polarized age where an "us versus them" mentality can convince us that those unlike ourselves are of less worth, this project is anchored in the belief that every human being is knit together by the same God and, as such, is of worth: a gift from God with gifts to share. This project affirms God as the giver of all good gifts, including the gifts of self, others, and the community we share. Its goal is to encourage people to voluntarily and collectively use their God-given gifts, even if they don't recognize their source, for the common good of their neighborhoods, loving their neighbors as themselves and working together to imagine the God-given possibilities.

1. Tony found that sometimes Christians can be isolated from or even dismissive of the place and people around them. What examples have you seen of this tendency?

2. The Hopeful Neighborhood Project is anchored in the belief that "every human being is knit together by the same God." How well does this belief sync with how you typically think of the non-Christians around you?

3. Spend some time learning about the Hopeful Neighborhood Project at hopefulneighborhood.org. What stands out to you or surprises you about this new network?

---

[a]Tony Cook and Don Everts, *The Hopeful Neighborhood Field Guide: Six Lessons on Pursuing the Common Good Right Where You Live* (Downers Grove, IL: InterVarsity Press, 2021).

Tony and his friends at the Hopeful Neighborhood Project are experiencing something that has been somewhat absent from the Western church in recent decades: hope. During our tough seasons, hope is a wonderful gift. While many things make Christians stand out from our surrounding culture "in these days in which we live, hope marks us out more dramatically, perhaps, than anything else."[16] As we look forward to that sure day when God's kingdom will be fully consummated in a new creation, we develop a "truer vision and fiercer hope."[17] And as we actually labor with others for that kingdom our hope only grows. Learning about how we are created to pursue the common good is one thing, but to join together with a few other people and risk creating something good together is another entirely.[18]

When we look back at momentous changes in history, we tend to focus on heroic individuals. When we think of the abolition of slavery in the United Kingdom, we remember William Wilberforce. When we think of the suffrage movement, we remember Susan B. Anthony. When we think of the civil rights movement in America, we remember Martin Luther King Jr. But the reality is each of these individuals was a part of a movement, a network of people. History-altering changes like these happen because of such organized networks, because of "millions of decisions made by ordinary people who wanted to see their country change."[19] This is the reality behind the most powerful social media movements and is one of the unique features of the few stories we've considered so far.

Greg Russinger didn't just help one homeless man in Ventura, California, who needed his clothes cleaned. Greg and his friends started Laundry Love, and a network spread across the United States.

Rebekah Morris didn't just empower one family living in an apartment complex in Atlanta. Rebekah and her students started Los Vecinos De Buford Highway, and a network spread to apartment complexes all along that road.

Jessica Crye didn't just give a kind gift to a renowned atheist in Henderson County, Texas. Jessica and her friends started an outpouring of generosity that spread throughout the county.

Sarah Bernhardt didn't just create a mosaic out of broken glass with her neighbors in Gravois Park, Missouri. Sarah and her neighbors started Intersect Arts Center, a collaborative effort that is drawing people and groups and government agencies together from throughout the St. Louis area.

And Tony Cook didn't just join with friends in pursuing the common good in his neighborhood. Tony and his friends started the Hopeful Neighborhood Project, a network that is helping people all across the country join together with their friends in pursuing the common good right where they live.

And this is reason for hope: to feel this ancient, long-dormant hunger inside of you to join with others in a grand mission. To feel that hunger begin to rumble and stir inside your gut. It's enough to make you want to join the revolution.

And that, as we get ready to set this book aside, is what I pray we all turn our attention to next.

Just as my friend Troy invited me to join a revolution all those years ago, I invite you to do the same. Just imagine . . .

What if we didn't just read about this hopeful revolution but actually joined it?

- Join me and Tony and all our friends in the Hopeful Neighborhood Project by visiting hopefulneighborhood.org.
- Learn how to pursue the common good right where you live by working through *The Hopeful Neighborhood Field Guide*.[20]

# Conclusion

## THIS LITTLE PATCH OF GROUND

Recently I was returning from a walk around my neighborhood and I saw Michael, my next-door neighbor, raking his leaves. He waved and I walked over, and we started another one of our unhurried philosophical life conversations we tend to have while standing on our front lawns. He was leaning on his rake and smiling as we talked.

I felt two things as we talked. On the one hand, I felt the blessing of knowing and being known by my neighbor. I'm no character in a Wendell Berry novel, but even I feel how right it is to have a relationship with the place and people around me.

On the other hand, I felt sobered again by how inattentive to my neighborhood I've grown over this last stretch of years. I felt that maybe I've taken something from Michael and the rest of my neighbors by growing so inattentive to Pierremont. And I wondered what all I've missed out on by not interacting more with Michael and the uniquely gifted people throughout my neighborhood.

When I was first swarmed by all those wonderful and pesky questions back in that hay maze in Tennessee, I felt a profound curiosity, as I've mentioned. But what I haven't mentioned yet is I also felt a nagging doubt. The curiosity was specific: as Christians, how should we interact with the place and people around us? That curiosity is what launched me on this wonderful journey of study, research, introspection, and action.

But at the beginning there was this nagging doubt I couldn't shake: even if we *should* pursue the common good of our neighborhoods, *could* we? I felt doubt because there are so many understandable reasons for us not to: we're too busy, we're focused on raising our kids, we're focused on personal spiritual growth, we don't have a passion for our neighborhoods, and maybe we don't want to hurt our local church by spending our energies elsewhere. Just to name a few barriers.

But along the way this doubt has begun to erode. It's not that we aren't busy or preoccupied with our kids or focusing on our own growth—often we are. And it's true we sometimes lack passion for our neighborhoods and don't want to detract from church programs. But, on closer inspection, none of those barriers amount to much. The research is pretty unambiguous on this:

- Too busy? The research shows that busier people are just as likely, if not *more* so, to be involved in their communities, compared to those with time on their hands.[1]

- Kids in the way? The latest findings tell us that parents of kids ages six to twelve are more likely than people with grown children to be active in pursuing the common good.[2]

- Personal growth instead? It turns out people who spend time blessing their local community grow spiritually and wind up feeling closer to God as a result.[3]

- No passion? Not surprisingly, the research suggests that joining with others for the sake of your neighborhood results in inspiration.[4]

- Don't want to hurt your church? You may find it encouraging that church programs do not suffer from a trade-off when people get involved in their neighborhoods. In fact, most pastors are happy to encourage lay-led initiatives over church programs for serving the community.[5]

Handling all this research has served to erode some of my doubts. And my time spent in the pages of Scripture and annals of church history have further eroded those initial doubts. I've become thoroughly convinced through God's Word that we are all beautifully created, explicitly called, and graciously reminded to pursue the common good right where we live. And I've been genuinely inspired by stories of Christians in much harsher times than our own doing just that in ways that were beautiful, rewarding, and intriguing to the world around them.

The truth is, after all this study and research and introspection, most of my doubts are simply gone. They are being replaced by a "living hope," as Peter put it in that letter to believers in Asia Minor. I see this beautiful, ancient path in front of me.

It's the same path in front of all of us: the path from division to unity and from irrelevance to relevance. This path leads to a more grounded and integrated way of life, to a kinder and more respectful way of influencing the world, to a more compelling and attractive Christian presence in our country, to greater use of the gifts God has given us, and to more genuine relationships with the non-Christians in our lives. This path starts right at our front doors and leads, by God's guidance and grace, to the place and people around us.

As we've seen, there's nothing new about this path—it's an ancient, well-worn way. It may appear radical in our age of division, self-protection, and inattentiveness to our neighbors, but there's nothing too novel or complicated about it. It's a simple path from you to the neighborhood you live in. The reality is, no matter where you live, you live in a neighborhood. And God just might be inviting you to pay more attention to that.

As for me and Wendy, our kids are swiftly graduating and launching out into the big, wide world. This naturally raises the question of whether we should stay here in Pierremont (my thirtieth neighborhood) or strategically relocate as empty nesters (and move to my thirty-first neighborhood). We haven't answered that question yet and are in no hurry to do so. But no matter how we answer that question, we know this: wherever we live, we want to live there. We don't want to "live above place" anymore. And we know we need help with this. That's why Wendy and I have joined the Hopeful Neighborhood Project.

Whatever neighborhood we live in, we want it to be a hopeful neighborhood. We want to do our hospitality thing and invite people over for meals and have our home be a knockabout place for folks in the neighborhood. We want to join with the neighbors God has given us and use our collective gifts together for the sake of the place and the people around us. And we don't want anyone in our neighborhood to ever go two decades without a handshake.

Wendy and I have joined our friends in the Hopeful Neighborhood Project because we want to live in a hopeful neighborhood. We invite you to join us there.

Maybe none of us are barbers like Jayber Crow of the novel I started reading in the center of a hay maze. But we are all a part of "the membership" of whatever neighborhood God has us in, whether we recognize that reality or not. As the character Jayber Crow put it,

> I have got to the age now where I can see how short a time we have to be here. And when I think about it, it can seem strange beyond telling that this particular bunch of us should be here on this little patch of ground in this little patch of time, and I can think of other times and places I might have lived, the other kinds of man I might have been. But then there is something else. There are moments when the heart is generous, and then it knows that for better or worse our lives are woven together here, one with one another and with the place and all the living things.[6]

As we close, I pray (borrowing from the barber): May God grant you the generosity of heart to know how your life is woven together with "the membership" of the little patch of ground he's placed you on. May God help you use the short time he's given you to do what he's created you for. And may God grow a harvest of hope within you and your neighborhood.

# Acknowledgments

I t has not escaped my attention that for a nomad to write a helpful and honest book about being a neighbor, a great deal of help must have been required. And it was.

This help has included the research savvy of the team at the Barna Group, the intellectual curiosity of the team at Lutheran Hour Ministries, the editorial excellence of Al Hsu at InterVarsity Press, the at-a-slant vision of Tony Cook, and the gracious guidance of Jason Broge. Oh, also the patience of family and friends engaged in my nonstop ponderous conversations about neighborhoods and farming and urbanism and theology and Wendell Berry. And then there's God's grace, of course. Yes, there's been lots of help along the way.

I find myself particularly thankful for all the neighbors and friends and family who have undoubtedly suffered because of my twitchy nomadic habits through the years but have nevertheless welcomed me into their hearts and lives and neighborhoods. I may not deserve their hospitality, but I receive it with gratitude.

# Appendix 1
## RESEARCH PARTNERS

### BARNA GROUP

**Barna Group** (barna.com) is a research firm dedicated to providing actionable insights on faith and culture, with a particular focus on the Christian church. Since 1984, Barna has conducted more than one million interviews in the course of hundreds of studies and has become a go-to source for organizations that want to better understand a complex and changing world from a faith perspective.

### LUTHERAN HOUR MINISTRIES

**Lutheran Hour Ministries** (lhm.org) is a trusted expert in global media that equips and engages a vibrant volunteer base to passionately proclaim the gospel to more than 100 million people worldwide each week. Through its headquarters in St. Louis, Missouri, and ministry centers on six continents, LHM reaches into more than fifty countries, often bringing Christ to places where no other Christian evangelistic organizations are present.

LHM and Barna are partnering on a three-year research endeavor to reveal how Americans are expressing their faith. The first year of research looked at how individuals engage in spiritual conversations—for more on these findings you can read *The Reluctant Witness: Discovering the Delight of Spiritual Conversations*. The second year of research looked at the influence of households on spiritual development—see *The Spiritually Vibrant Home: The Power of Messy Prayers, Loud Tables, and Open Doors* for more on this study. The third year, which *The Hopeful Neighborhood* is based on, focuses on the impact of Christians on the broader community.

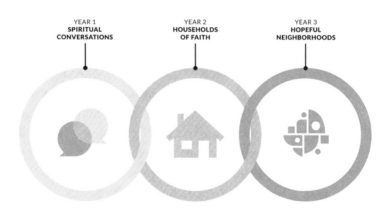

YEAR 1
**SPIRITUAL CONVERSATIONS**

YEAR 2
**HOUSEHOLDS OF FAITH**

YEAR 3
**HOPEFUL NEIGHBORHOODS**

# Appendix 2
## RESEARCH METHODOLOGY

This quantitative study consisted of two online surveys. The first was a survey of 2,500 US adults conducted July 25–August 19, 2019. The sample included 1,505 US practicing Christians (meaning they self-identify as Christian, say their faith is very important in their life, and have attended church within the past month other than for a holiday service or for a special event, such as a wedding or funeral). The margin of error for this sample is + /- 1.7 percent at the 95 percent confidence level.

Researchers set quotas to obtain a minimum readable sample by a variety of demographic factors and weighted the general population data by region, ethnicity, education, age, and gender to reflect their natural presence in the American population (using US Census Bureau data for comparison). Partly by the nature of using an online panel, these respondents are slightly more educated than the average American, but Barna researchers adjusted the representation of college-educated individuals in the weighting scheme accordingly.

The second quantitative online survey was conducted among 508 US Protestant senior pastors on July 25-August 13,

2019. These pastors were recruited from Barna's pastor panel (a database of pastors recruited via probability sampling on annual phone and email surveys) and are representative of US Protestant churches by region, denomination, and church size. The margin of error for this sample is + /- 4.2 percent at the 95 percent confidence level.

This study also included ethnographic research and qualitative interviews with eighteen individuals who had some kind of experience working with community groups and organizations. These interviews, conducted July–September 2019, used a flexible script to learn how such groups form, how they work, and what makes them effective.[1]

# Appendix 3
## DEFINITIONS

**Practicing Christians** are self-identified Christians who say their faith is very important in their lives and have attended a worship service within the past month.

**Group participants** at some time in their adulthood have had the following experiences in some kind of group, club, or other association:

- Their participation was not required for their education or schooling.

- Their participation was not directly related to their job.

- The group included three or more people.

- The group met three or more times.

- The group provided some external benefits reaching beyond its participants. Though those benefits might have extended widely, they had to have some local impact, meaning in one's city or town. Additionally, while a church or Christian community could have benefitted, it could not have been the only beneficiary of the group's actions.[1]

# Notes

**INTRODUCTION: LIVING ABOVE PLACE**

[1]Paul Sparks, Tim Soerens, and Dwight J. Friesen, *The New Parish: How Neighborhood Churches Are Transforming Mission, Discipleship and Community* (Downers Grove, IL: InterVarsity Press, 2014), 24.

[2]Don Everts, *The Reluctant Witness: Discovering the Delight of Spiritual Conversations* (Downers Grove, IL: InterVarsity Press, 2019).

[3]Don Everts, *The Spiritually Vibrant Home: The Power of Messy Prayers, Loud Tables, and Open Doors* (Downers Grove, IL: InterVarsity Press, 2020).

[4]Barna Group, *Better Together: How Christians Can Be a Welcome Influence in Their Neighborhoods* (Ventura, CA: Barna Groups, 2020).

[5]John McKnight and Peter Block, *The Abundant Community: Awakening the Power of Families and Neighborhoods* (Oakland, CA: Berrett-Koehler, 2010), 5.

**1 PURSUE THE COMMON GOOD**

[1]See John E. Hartley, *Genesis*, New International Biblical Commentary (Peabody, MA: Hendrickson, 2000), 59; and Franz Delitzsch, *A New Commentary on Genesis* (Eugene, OR: Wipf & Stock, 2001), 1:137.

[2]Victor P. Hamilton, *The Book of Genesis: Chapters 1-17*, The New International Commentary on the Old Testament (Grand Rapids: Eerdmans, 1990), 171.

[3]Hamilton, *Book of Genesis*, 171.

[4]Hartley, *Genesis*, 60; and Hamilton, *Book of Genesis*, 171.

[5]Eric O. Jacobsen, *The Space Between: A Christian Engagement with the Built Environment* (Grand Rapids: Baker, 2012), 20.

[6]Jake Meador, *In Search of the Common Good: Christian Fidelity in a Fractured World* (Downers Grove, IL: InterVarsity Press, 2019), 29.

[7]Walter Brueggemann, *Journey to the Common Good* (Louisville, KY: Westminster John Knox Press, 2010), 1.

[8]C. John Collins, *Genesis 1–4: A Linguistic, Literary, and Theological Commentary* (Phillipsburg, NJ: P&R, 2006), 69.

[9]Andy Crouch, *Playing God: Redeeming the Gift of Power* (Downers Grove, IL: InterVarsity Press, 2013), 35.

[10]Crouch, *Playing God*, 17.

[11]Collins, *Genesis 1–4*, 165.

[12]Timothy Keller, *Generous Justice: How God's Grace Makes Us Just* (New York: Penguin Random House, 2012), 170.

[13]James Davison Hunter, *To Change the World: The Irony, Tragedy, and Possibility of Christianity in the Late Modern World* (New York: Oxford University Press, 2010), 4.

[14]See Appendix 3: Definitions.

[15]Barna Group, *Better Together: How Christians Can Be a Welcome Influence in Their Neighborhoods* (Ventura, CA: Barna Group, 2020), 63.

[16]Barna, *Better Together*, 63.

[17]Paul Sparks, Tim Soerens, and Dwight J. Friesen, *The New Parish: How Neighborhood Churches Are Transforming Mission, Discipleship and Community* (Downers Grove, IL: InterVarsity Press, 2014), 23.

[18]Jim Wallis, *The (Un)Common Good: How the Gospel Brings Hope to a World Divided* (Grand Rapids: Brazos, 2013), 277.

[19]Hunter, *Change the World*, 281.

[20]Barna, *Better Together*, 43.

## 2 USE EVERY GIFT

[1]Franz Delitzsch, *A New Commentary on Genesis* (Eugene, OR: Wipf & Stock, 2001), 1:101.

[2]Victor P. Hamilton, *The Book of Genesis: Chapters 1-17,* The New International Commentary on the Old Testament (Grand Rapids: Eerdmans, 1990), 138.

[3]William L Holladay, *A Concise Hebrew and Aramaic Lexicon of the Old Testament* (Grand Rapids: Eerdmans, 1972).

[4]James Davison Hunter, *To Change the World: The Irony, Tragedy, and Possibility of Christianity in the Late Modern World* (New York: Oxford University Press, 2010), 232.

[5]C. John Collins, *Genesis 1–4: A Linguistic, Literary, and Theological Commentary* (Phillipsburg, NJ: P&R, 2006), 107.

[6]Delitzsch, *New Commentary on Genesis,* 140.

[7]Martin Luther, *Small Catechism* (St. Louis, MO: Concordia Publishing House, 1971), 91.

[8]Hunter, *Change the World,* 232.

[9]See, for example, Douglas A. Hall, *The Cat and the Toaster: Living System Ministry in a Technological Age* (Eugene, OR: Wipf & Stock, 2010).

[10]John McKnight and Peter Block, *The Abundant Community: Awakening the Power of Families and Neighborhoods* (Oakland, CA: Berrett-Koehler, 2010), 71.

[11]See, for example, John P. Pretzmann and John L. McKnight, *Building Communities from the Inside Out: A Path Toward Finding and Mobilizing a Community's Assets* (Evanston, IL: Center for Urban Affairs and Policy Research, Northwestern University, 1993).

[12]McKnight and Block, *Abundant Community,* 70.

[13]Tony Cook and Don Everts, *The Hopeful Neighborhood Field Guide: Six Lessons on Pursuing the Common Good Right Where You Live* (Downers Grove, IL: InterVarsity Press, 2021).

[14]Gene Edward Veith, *Working for Our Neighbor: A Lutheran Primer on Vocation, Economics, and Ordinary Life* (Grand Rapids, MI: Christian's Library Press, 2016), xvi, 14.

[15]Makoto Fujimura, *Culture Care: Reconnecting with Beauty for Our Common Life* (Downers Grove, IL: InterVarsity Press, 2017), 83.

[16]Hunter, *Change the World,* 3-4.

[17]David Kinnaman and Mark Matlock, *Faith for Exiles: 5 Ways for a New Generation to Follow Jesus in Digital Babylon* (Grand Rapids: Baker, 2019), 155.

[18]McKnight and Block, *Abundant Community,* 1.

[19]Peter Block, *Community: The Structure of Belonging* (Oakland, CA: Berrett-Koehler, 2018), 13-14.

## 3 LOVE EVERYONE ALWAYS

[1]Francis A. Schaeffer, *Genesis in Space and* Time (Downers Grove, IL: InterVarsity Press, 1972), 47.

[2]John Calvin, *Genesis* (Wheaton, IL: Crossway, 2001), 37.

[3]Calvin, *Genesis,* 27.

[4]Schaeffer, *Genesis in Space and Time,* 116.

[5]Karen H. Jobes, *1 Peter,* Baker Exegetical Commentary on the New Testament (Grand Rapids: Baker Academic, 2005), 217.

[6]Jobes, *1 Peter,* 171.

[7]Suetonius's *Nero* and Tacitus's *Annals,* quoted in Jobes, *1 Peter,* 171.

[8]Jobes, *1 Peter,* 168.

[9]Jobes, *1 Peter,* 218.

[10]Curtis Chang, *Engaging Unbelief: A Captivating Strategy from Augustine and Aquinas* (Downers Grove, IL: InterVarsity Press, 2000), 19.

[11]David Kinnaman and Mark Matlock, *Faith for Exiles: 5 Ways for a New Generation to Follow Jesus in Digital Babylon* (Grand Rapids: Baker, 2019), 20-21.

[12]Jake Meador, *In Search of the Common Good: Christian Fidelity in a Fractured World* (Downers Grove, IL: InterVarsity Press, 2019), 10.

[13]Meador, *Search of the Common Good,* 10.

[14]Barna Group, *Spiritual Conversations in the Digital Age: How Christians' Approach to Sharing Their Faith Has Changed in 25 Years* (Ventura, CA: Barna Group, 2018), 10.

[15]Chang, *Engaging Unbelief,* 19.

[16]James Davison Hunter, *To Change the World: The Irony, Tragedy, and Possibility of Christianity in the Late Modern World* (New York: Oxford University Press, 2010), 107.

[17]See Don Everts, *The Reluctant Witness: Discovering the Delight of Spiritual Conversations* (Downers Grove, IL: InterVarsity Press, 2019).

[18]Walter Brueggemann, *Texts Under Negotiation: The Bible and Postmodern Imagination* (Minneapolis: Fortress Press, 1993), 18.

[19]Christian Smith, *American Evangelicalism: Embattled and Thriving* (Chicago: University of Chicago Press, 1998), 140ff.

[20]Hunter, *Change the World,* 167.

[21]Makoto Fujimura, *Culture Care: Reconnecting with Beauty for Our Common Life* (Downers Grove, IL: InterVarsity Press, 2017), 39.

## 4 GIVE GOD GLORY

[1]W. E. Vine, *An Expository Dictionary of New Testament Words* (Old Tappan, NJ: Fleming H. Revell, 1966), 153-155.

[2]Francis A. Schaeffer, *Genesis in Space and Time* (Downers Grove, IL: InterVarsity Press, 1972), 56.

[3]See Don Everts, *The Reluctant Witness: Discovering the Delight of Spiritual Conversations* (Downers Grove, IL: InterVarsity Press, 2019).

[4]Karen H. Jobes, *1 Peter,* Baker Exegetical Commentary on the New Testament (Grand Rapids: Baker Academic, 2005), 217.

[5]Jim Wallis, *The (Un)Common Good: How the Gospel Brings Hope to a World Divided* (Grand Rapids: Brazos, 2013), xiii.

[6]Barna Group, *Better Together: How Christians Can Be a Welcome Influence in Their Neighborhoods* (Ventura, CA: Barna Groups, 2020), 73.

[7]Wallis, *(Un)Common Good*, 6.

[8]Wallis, *(Un)Common Good*, 279.

## 5 JOIN THE REVOLUTION

[1]C. John Collins, *Genesis 1–4: A Linguistic, Literary, and Theological Commentary* (Phillipsburg, NJ: P&R, 2006), 69.

[2]Eric O. Jacobsen, *The Space Between: A Christian Engagement with the Built Environment* (Grand Rapids: Baker Academic, 2012), 118.

[3]Wayne Grudem, *1 Peter,* Tyndale New Testament Commentaries (Grand Rapids: Eerdmans, 1988), 37; Edmund Clowney, *The Message of 1 Peter,* The Bible Speaks Today Series (Downers Grove, IL: Inter-Varsity Press, 2014), 17.

[4]Barbara Friberg, Neva F. Mille, and Timothy Friberg, *Analytical Lexicon of the Greek New Testament* (Bloomington, IN: Trafford, 2006).

[5]Frederick William Danker, *The Concise Greek-English Lexicon of the New Testament* (Chicago: University of Chicago Press, 2009).

[6]Barna Group, *Better Together: How Christians Can Be a Welcome Influence in Their Neighborhoods* (Ventura, CA: Barna Group, 2020), 97.

[7]July 25–August 19, 2019 quantitative survey, see Appendix 2.

[8]Barna, *Better Together*, 97.

[9]Kevin J. Vanhoozer, *The Drama of Doctrine: A Canonical Linguistic Approach to Christian Doctrine* (Louisville, KY: Westminster John Knox Press, 2005), 454.

[10]James Davison Hunter, *To Change the World: The Irony, Tragedy, and Possibility of Christianity in the Late Modern World* (New York: Oxford University Press, 2010), 271.

[11]Andy Crouch, *Playing God: Redeeming the Gift of Power* (Downers Grove, IL: InterVarsity Press, 2013), 169.

[12]Hunter, *Change the World,* 270.

[13]Crouch, *Playing God,* 188.

[14]Hunter, *Change the World,* 38.

[15]Hunter, *Change the World,* 270, 38.

[16]Roy Clements, *Faithful Living in a Faithless World* (Downers Grove, IL: InterVarsity Press, 1998), 163.

[17]Douglas Kain McKelvey, *Every Moment Holy* (Nashville: Rabbit Room Press, 2017), 98.

[18]Andy Crouch, *Culture Making: Recovering Our Creative Calling* (Downers Grove, IL: InterVarsity Press, 2008), 247.

[19]Jim Wallis, *The (Un)Common Good: How the Gospel Brings Hope to a World Divided* (Grand Rapids: Brazos, 2013), 291.

[20]Tony Cook and Don Everts, *The Hopeful Neighborhood Field Guide: Six Lessons on Pursuing the Common Good Right Where You Live* (Downers Grove, IL: InterVarsity Press, 2021).

## CONCLUSION: THIS LITTLE PATCH OF GROUND

[1]Barna Group, *Better Together: How Christians Can Be a Welcome Influence in Their Neighborhoods* (Ventura, CA: Barna Group, 2020), 27.

[2]Barna, *Better Together,* 27.

[3]Barna, *Better Together,* 85.

[4]Barna, *Better Together,* 57.

[5]Barna, *Better Together,* 95, 83.

[6]Wendell Berry, *Jayber Crow: The Life Story of Jayber Crow, Barber, of the Port William Membership, as Written by Himself* (Berkeley, CA: Counterpoint Press, 2000), 210.

## APPENDIX 2: RESEARCH METHODOLOGY

[1]Barna Group, *Better Together: How Christians Can Be a Welcome Influence in Their Neighborhoods* (Ventura, CA: Barna Group, 2020), 107-8.

## APPENDIX 3: DEFINITIONS

[1]Barna Group, *Better Together: How Christians Can Be a Welcome Influence in Their Neighborhoods* (Ventura, CA: Barna Group, 2020), 108.

THE **HOPEFUL**
**NEIGHBORHOOD**
**PROJECT** ®

The Hopeful Neighborhood Project is a collaborative network committed to improving neighborhood well-being around the world. Our resources and online network equip and encourage neighbors to work together, using their gifts and the gifts of their community, to pursue the common good of their neighborhood.

*To find out more about our*
*active network and many resources visit us at*
**hopefulneighborhood.org.**

# Other Titles by Don Everts

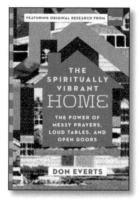

*The Spiritually Vibrant Home*
978-0-8308-4590-3

*The Reluctant Witness*
978-0-8308-4567-5

*Breaking the Huddle*
978-0-8308-4491-3

*I Once Was Lost*
978-0-8308-3608-6